AACRAO®
1 9 1 0

APPLYING

SEM

AT THE

COMMUNITY
COLLEGE

edited by

Bob Bontrager & Bruce Clemetsen

Sponsored by SUNGARD® HIGHER EDUCATION

American Association of Collegiate
Registrars and Admissions Officers
One Dupont Circle, NW, Suite 520
Washington, DC 20036–1135

Tel: (202) 293–9161 | Fax: (202) 872–8857 | www.aacrao.org

For a complete listing of AACRAO publications, visit www.aacrao.org/publications.

The American Association of Collegiate Registrars and Admissions Officers, founded
in 1910, is a nonprofit, voluntary, professional association of more than 10,000 higher
education administrators who represent more than 2,600 institutions and agencies in the
United States and in twenty-eight countries around the world. The mission of the Association is to provide leadership in policy initiation, interpretation, and implementation
in the global educational community. This is accomplished through the identification
and promotion of standards and best practices in enrollment management, information
technology, instructional management, and student services.

LIBRARY OF CONGRESS CATALOGING-IN-PUBLICATION DATA

Applying SEM at the community college / Bob Bontrager,
    Bruce Clemetsen, editors.

  p. cm.

ISBN 978-1-57858-089-7

1. Community colleges—United States—Business management.
2. Community colleges—United States—Finance.
3. College attendance—United States—Planning.

I.   Bontrager, Bob.
II. Clemetsen, Bruce.
III. Title: Applying strategic enrollment management at the
     community college.

LB2341.93.U6A66 2009
378.1'06—dc22
2009035068

CONTENTS

Preface..i

The Authors iii

1 Strategic Enrollment Management at Community Colleges I

by Bob Bontrager and Kevin Pollock

SEM Defined...3

    Establishing Comprehensive Enrollment Goals 4

    Promoting Academic Success..5

    Promoting Institutional Success 5

    Creating A Data-Rich Environment 6

    Strengthening Internal and External Communications 6

    Increasing Campus Collaboration 6

SEM in Two-Year Institutions...7

    Diverse Student Body 7

    Specialized Student Challenges..8

    Multiple Goals 9

2 What is a Successful Community College Student?.. I I

by Bruce Clemetsen and Jeff Rhodes

Defining and Measuring Student Success.. 18

    Models for Defining Success Metrics.. 18

Comprehensive Views of Student Success.. 20

    Measuring Student Success.. 25

Advising as the Keystone to Student Success... 28

3 Strategic Enrollment Management and Instructional Division 33

by Bruce Clemetsen

Connecting SEM to the Institutional Core of Teaching and Learning........................... 35

CCSSE and SENSE: Foundations for Engaging Faculty in SEM 38

An Academic Orientation to SEM 44

Instructional Involvement in SEM Systems 46

    Recruitment.. 46

Admission Standards for Limited Enrollment Programs..47

Scholarships 47

Prerequisites...48

Early Alert Systems 48

Course Scheduling 48

Co-curricular Programs..49

4 Data and Decision Making..51

by Christine Kerlin and William Serrata

The Case for Using Data..53

Data Collection 54

Data Accuracy and Relevance 56

Collecting Data..57

   Environmental Scan 57

   Factbook 58

   Dashboard 58

   Key Performance Indicators..58

   Benchmarking..59

   Special Reports 59

Data Tools..60

Data Analysis...61

Data Dangers...63

   The Data Cycle..63

   Analysis Paralysis...64

   Data Detachment..65

5 Building Effective Community College/University Partnerships................67

by Bruce Clemetsen

The Importance of Partnerships to Community Colleges...70

Partnerships and SEM..71

The Community College–University Partnership...73

6 Marketing Community Colleges..81

by Alicia Moore and Ron Paradis

Understanding the Marketing Mix...84

Product 85

Price...88

Place...90

Promotion..91

People...93

7 Supporting a SEM Plan: Role of Technology 95

by Wendy Kilgore and Kenneth Sharp

Technology and a SEM Environment Scan 99

External Scan 99

Internal Scan 105

Technology and SEM Efforts 106

Measuring Technological Competence 107

Recruiting and Admissions Technologies 108

Pre-Enrollment and Enrollment Technologies 112

Retention Technologies 114

Degree Completion Technologies 117

Successful Selection and Implementation of Technology 119

Post-Implementation Considerations 120

8 Developing and Implementing a Student Recruitment Plan 123

by Bruce Clemetsen and Dennis Bailey-Fougnier

Evolution of Community College Recruitment 126

Developing a Recruitment Plan 128

Relating Recruitment to the Strategic Plan and Academic Master Plan 129

Collecting Critical Data to Shape the Plan 129

Finding Supportive Allies 130

Determining Institutional Strengths 131

Determining Competition for Market Niches and Programs 131

Scanning for New Opportunities 132

Setting Targets 132

Feedback Loops 133

Core Recruitment Practices 133

The Enrollment Funnel 133

The Communication Plan 136

Recruitment Plan Realities 137

9 Strategic Enrollment Management's Financial Dynamics 143

by Kenneth Sharp

Why Worry about SEM and Community Colleges? 145

Higher Education Finances 147

A SEM Perspective on Budgeting 148

Sources of Revenues 149

Tuition and Fees 149

State Appropriations 151

Local Taxes 151
Cost Concepts 152
Marginal Costs vs. Average Costs 152
Facilities Costs 153
Demand/Enrollment 153
Identifying SEM Investments and Measurable Outcomes 154
Implementing the SEM Planning Model 155
Phase 1: Developing Comprehensive Enrollment Goals 155
Phase 2: Identifying Strategic Enrollment Investments and Measurable Outcomes 156
Phase 3: Tracking Enrollment, Net Revenue, and Budget Outcomes 157
Phase 4: Creating Reinvestment Strategies 157
SEM Financial Planning in Action 159
Phase 1: Developing Comprehensive Enrollment Goals 159
Phase 2: Identifying Strategic Enrollment Investments and Measurable Outcomes 160
Phase 3: Tracking Enrollment, Net Revenue and Budget Outcomes 163
Phase 4: Creating Reinvestment Strategies 163

10 Strategic Enrollment Management and Campus Leadership 167

by Christine Kerlin and William Serrata

The Case for Leadership 169
Leadership Ingredients 172
Building a Leadership Approach 174
Leading SEM 176
Development 176
Implementation 177
Assessment and Revitalization 178

11 Implementing SEM at the Community College 181

by Bob Bontrager and Alicia Moore

Clear Mission and Goals 184
Data Collection and Analysis 185
Enrollment Infrastructure 186
Implementing SEM: A Case Study 189
Setting the Stage 190
Establishing a SEM Team 192
Clear Mission and Goals 193
Data Review and Goal Development 194
Enrollment Infrastructure 196

References 199

PREFACE

Are we entering a "golden age" for community colleges?

As this volume goes to press, we are witness to an unprecedented confluence of events. With a renewed focus on the role of community colleges in education and workforce development, the promise of significant funding through the Obama administration's American Graduation Initiative, and Dr. Jill Biden's compelling support—at home and abroad—for the community college mission, a golden age seems quite possible. This uniquely American education system, founded on open access and innovative in its reach, has helped thousands of students find their way toward the American dream.

President Obama's pledge to reform and strengthen our community colleges so that five million more students in the next decade can have access to the education they need will revitalize how we think about the community college movement and its traditional mission of open access. If our schools can find no way to accommodate the sheer numbers of students eager to walk through their doors and help them define and achieve their education and job-related goals, the potential of this transformative moment will be lost.

That is why I am so pleased that AACRAO asked SunGard Higher Education to sponsor *Applying Strategic Enrollment Management at the Community College*, a collection of essays that could not be timelier. It is our view that SEM, insofar as it embodies a philosophy of constituent engagement closely aligned with an institution's overarching mission, is, in many ways, already coded into the community college DNA. When done right, SEM can help an institution act more deliberately to target, engage, and support the students it serves—and seeks to serve. That twinning of access—reaching out effectively to the many diverse student cohorts your institution serves—and success—supporting them with the services they need to achieve their goals—has always been at the heart of the community college mission.

The principles of SEM, as this volume makes clear, will help community colleges pursue this dual mission in a more focused and systematic way. In independent research conducted by SunGard Higher Education over the course of 2009, community college students identified balancing school with the demands of work, home, and finances as a significant hardship. Close on the heels of this fundamental challenge were concerns of a different order: concerns about course scheduling, remediation, academic planning and tracking, and transferring credits between colleges. With a strategic approach to the *full* student experience, institutions can identify and address all of these obstacles early and effectively, building a lifelong commitment to your institution and to the principles of the community college mission.

By 2020, your institution will experience more diversity in its student body than ever before. The business models of your corporate partners will be more dynamic. How we define and measure outcomes will be more transparent. And new technologies will continue to contribute to a more mobile teaching and learning infrastructure. Going forward, your challenge will be to manage that diversity and shape those myriad stakeholder needs into an engaged and participatory community.

That, I think, is the brilliance of this volume, which, to my mind, begins to redefine SEM in the context of a broader vision of outreach and engagement. By understanding SEM as a way to manage relationships among the many constituents with a stake in the community college enterprise, this volume points the way to true "constituent engagement management:" a more open and authentic engagement model, grounded in the student experience, that asks the fundamental question: how can we help you succeed?

How our community colleges answer that question over the next ten years will comprise a tapestry of ideas and initiatives. The promise of SEM, and the engagement models that evolve from it, is the promise of expectations fulfilled. With an enthusiastic community of support, our students will realize the kinds of successes that drive personal achievement and economic development. All of us here at SunGard Higher Education are proud to support that mission and wish you well on this amazing journey.

Fred B. Weiss
Senior Vice President, SunGard Higher Education

THE AUTHORS

Dennis Bailey-Fougnier

Dennis Bailey-Fougnier is the Vice President of Student Service at Cabrillo College in Aptos, California. Dennis has performed a variety of student services roles at both community colleges and universities. He currently is completing his dissertation on the effectiveness of degree partnership programs to increase bachelor's degree attainment for community college students.

Bob Bontrager

Bob Bontrager has 25 years of experience in enrollment management at many different types of colleges and universities, with expertise in strategic planning, recruitment, retention, financial aid, marketing, net revenue strategies, and educational partnerships. As Assistant Provost for Enrollment Management at Oregon State University, his efforts led to a 40 percent increase in enrollment. Dr. Bontrager is currently the Director of the AACRAO Strategic Enrollment Management Conference, and Director of AACRAO Consulting.

Bruce Clemetsen

Bruce Clemetsen serves as Dean of Student Services at Linn-Benton Community College in Albany, Oregon. Bruce has performed a variety of student services roles at multiple types of institutions. He also currently serves as a student services representative on the Oregon Student Success Indicator Oversight committee.

Christine Kerlin

Christine Kerlin is the Vice President for Enrollment Management and Executive Director of the University Center of North Puget Sound at Everett Community

College, Washington, and an AACRAO Consulting Senior Consultant. Dr. Kerlin is a nationally-known expert on enrollment management in community colleges with previous experience as Director of Admissions and Records at Central Oregon Community College and as Director of Admissions at The Evergreen State College, Washington. Her areas of experience include admissions, registration, records, international programs, credential evaluation, high school dual enrollment, placement testing, articulation, and strategic planning.

Wendy Kilgore

Wendy Kilgore is Dean of Enrollment Services for the Colorado Community College System. She served previously as Director of Admissions and Registrar for the Pima County Community College District in Tucson, Arizona, and a campus Director of Enrollment Services at Pima. She has also served as a Regional Coordinator for Undergraduate Admissions and as an Academic Advisor for Arizona State University. Her wide-ranging experience includes recruitment, admissions, financial aid, academic advising, records, curriculum support, veterans' education services, systems implementation, business practice improvements and reengineering, policy review and development, and building system-wide collaboration to support enrollment efforts.

Alicia Moore

Alicia Moore is the Dean of Student and Enrollment Services for Central Oregon Community College (cocc). She has over 14 years of experience in student services, and most recently, she served as the Director of Admissions/Registrar for cocc, where through her collaborative efforts the campus achieved a record 12 percent enrollment growth in just two years. During her tenure at cocc, Alicia's accomplishments include development of a comprehensive one-stop service center, including admissions, registration, student account/bursar and financial aid, placement testing, and academic advising.

Ron Paradis

Ron Paradis has been the Director of College Relations at Central Oregon Community College for 18 years. In this role, he oversees strategic communications, publications, media relations, internal communications, crisis communications and general community relations. He is actively involved in professional and community organizations.

Kevin Pollock

Dr. Kevin Pollock is the president at St. Clair County Community College in Port Huron, Michigan. Prior to this position he served in multiple student services roles at Kettering University, Lawrence Technological University, Lake Superior State University, and West Shore Community College. He is the author of over a dozen book chapters and articles and has spoken nationally at over sixty conferences and colleges on numerous enrollment management, student services, and student success topics.

Jeff Rhodes

Jeff Rhodes is the Dean of Enrollment Management at Southeastern Louisiana University in Hammond, Louisiana. Jeff served a number of years in community colleges and universities before taking on his current role. His research addresses issues of community college student transfer and factors influencing students' educational decisions and pathways to success.

William Serrata

William Serrata is the Vice-President for Student Affairs and Enrollment Management for South Texas College. His expertise includes strategic enrollment management, Hispanic student access and success within higher education, and student services' role in facilitating student success. The Commissioner of Texas Higher Education has appointed Mr. Serrata to serve on the Strategic Enrollment Management Committee. William serves on the Workforce Education Leadership Committee and has served on the Executive Committee for the Texas Association of Collegiate Registrars and Admissions Officers.

Kenneth Sharp

Ken Sharp serves as Assistant Director of Finance and Administration for Facilities at the University of Colorado, Denver. Prior to joining the University, he spent 16 years working in a variety of finance and administrative roles for community colleges at both the college and state level. Dr. Sharp's research has focused on cost structures among community colleges and the relationships between enrollments and college costs.

1

STRATEGIC ENROLLMENT MANAGEMENT AT
Community Colleges

by Bob Bontrager *and* Kevin Pollock

1 Strategic enrollment management, or SEM, has been part of the higher education landscape for more than thirty years. During that time, it has moved successively through various sectors of higher education, driven by demographic and economic forces that have led to a stark reality: the only way for most institutions to increase revenue in the current economic environment is to grow enrollments. Through the mid-1990s, community colleges were largely immune from this trend. Their multifaceted, community based, open door, and low cost approach to enrollment virtually assured a steady stream of students. In more recent years, and especially in the severe economic downturn of the late 2000s, community colleges—and many technical colleges—find themselves joining their four-year counterparts in embracing SEM as a conceptual framework for meeting today's enrollment and financial challenges. This chapter provides a definition of SEM and describes its application in the unique setting of two-year institutions.

SEM DEFINED

For the purposes of this book, we will define strategic enrollment management as *a concept and process that enables the fulfillment of institutional mission and students' educational goals*. In practice, the purposes of SEM are achieved by:

- Establishing comprehensive goals for the number and types of students needed to fulfill the institutional mission
- Promoting students' academic success by improving access, transition, persistence, and graduation

● Promoting institutional success by enabling effective strategic and financial planning
● Creating a data-rich environment to inform decisions and evaluate strategies
● Strengthening communications and marketing with internal and external stakeholders
● Increasing collaboration among departments across the campus to support the enrollment program

Establishing Comprehensive Enrollment Goals

Determining an institution's optimum enrollment profile is an extraordinarily complex undertaking, requiring careful and thorough analysis of multiple data points (Dolence 1993). The outcome is not one enrollment goal, but many. Depending on institutional type, the goals will address a wide range of student attributes. Examples include:

● Academic ability
● Academic program interest
● Race/ethnicity
● Geographic origin
● Undergraduate/graduate
● Degree completion
● Distance education
● Financial status
● Resident status
● Program and facility capacities
● Special skills (fine arts, leadership, athletics)
● Religious affiliation

Setting enrollment goals at this level of detail constitutes an intense and time-consuming process. Here the link between institutional mission and student profile becomes apparent, as different campus stakeholders express their varying perspectives on which students the institution should enroll and why. Given the inherent difficulties, institutions often attempt to skip over this stage of planning and move quickly to implement tactics they believe will increase the number of students recruited or retained. However, the failure to take adequate time to develop foundational goals results in diminished results at each subsequent stage of the strategic planning process (Bontrager 2008).

Promoting Academic Success

While mission-based enrollment goals form the foundation of SEM, it ultimately succeeds or fails based on the strength of its links to academics and student success. Whatever their broader purposes, institutional missions are based on the academic enterprise. Similarly, achieving enrollment goals depends on an institution's ability to promote students' academic success effectively. Delivering programs and building relationships that enhance students' access, transition, persistence, and goal attainment (degree or certificate completion, job skill enhancement, etc.) will determine the institution's ability to recruit and retain students in sufficient numbers to achieve desired enrollments.

From the institutional perspective, the vitality of the campus as a whole, as well as individual academic departments, depends on enrolling an adequate number of students. In advanced applications of SEM, recruitment and retention activities are coordinated at the departmental level. These program-specific efforts will shift over time in response to changing career opportunities, expansion into new geographic markets, and emergence of new niche opportunities where public demand and campus expertise converge. For all these reasons, it is critical to link SEM directly to an institution's academic mission and programs.

Promoting Institutional Success

In addition to fulfilling the mission by enrolling the optimal number and types of students, SEM can be a driver for more effective strategic and financial planning, achieved in large part by gaining clarity on comprehensive enrollment targets. Extending the planning horizon for enrollment goals provides even greater benefit. SEM encourages a shift from the backward-looking perspective of "how can we bring in more students than we had last year?" to the forward-looking orientation of "what is our desired future?"

For most institutions, the notion of achieving optimum enrollment represents a significant shift from the status quo. For that reason, it is useful to push the planning horizon out to ten years. This allows an institution to prioritize and plan investments aimed at enrolling specific target groups of students, with the initiatives implemented in stages over a reasonable time period. In so doing, the campus can avoid the common pitfall of attempting to achieve enrollment goals for each of their target groups simultaneously.

Creating A Data-Rich Environment

SEM is a performance-based, outcomes-oriented enterprise that requires copious amounts of data to operate effectively. While referred to in a variety of ways—performance indicators, success indicators, and outcomes assessment to name a few—SEM relies on a broad array of metrics to assess the achievement of goals, evaluate program effectiveness, and benchmark operations and strategies with other institutions. In the absence of hard data, enrollment decision-making will depend on anecdotes and hunches, with final decisions dictated by the opinion of the highest-ranked person in the discussion. Decisions made in this way will not achieve the desired outcomes.

Strengthening Internal and External Communications

A commonly understood and crucial component of SEM is marketing. Indeed, virtually every SEM plan includes specific initiatives for communicating effectively with prospective students, parents, community members, alumni, and other external stakeholders. In addition, SEM promotes stronger communication to internal stakeholders as well. Internal communications is critical given the mission-based nature of SEM. As such, SEM planning must engage every member of the campus community. This holds true during the crafting of enrollment goals, as well as when decisions are made regarding enrollment targets and related financial implications.

Increasing Campus Collaboration

SEM depends on the creation of strong and effective working relationships with virtually every department on campus. Effective recruitment and retention hinge on a series of individual encounters that ultimately define the quality of the student experience. These potential encounters range from an advising appointment with a professor, to an interaction with a receptionist, to the ability of a prospective student to find a parking spot. Communicating enrollment goals and assisting each member of the campus community to understand her or his role in achieving them can avoid negative student experiences. This requires formalized communication and feedback loops.

SEM IN TWO-YEAR INSTITUTIONS

As the utilization of SEM in community and technical colleges setting increases, there is a growing realization that the concept, implementation, and scope of SEM in two-year institutions can be vastly different for enrollment managers than that of their counterparts at four-year schools. Reflecting these differences, Christine Kerlin (2008), vice president for enrollment management and executive director of the University Center of North Puget Sound at Everett Community College in Washington developed this definition of enrollment management for community and technical colleges:

> *Enrollment management is a comprehensive and coordinated process that enables a college to identify enrollment goals that are allied with its multiple missions, its strategic plan, its environment, and its resources, and to reach those goals through the effective integration of administrative processes, student services, curriculum planning, and market analysis* (p. 11).

Building from this definition, the implications of practicing SEM in community colleges are further described below.

Diverse Student Body

A major initiative of SEM involves creating comprehensive goals for the number and types of students. This might be easier for four-year institutions where the bulk of the student population is "traditional" and usually comes directly from high school. What types of students attend community colleges? Besides the "traditional" students, they are older, have been away from academic settings longer, and come from lower socioeconomic settings. Consider the following data from "Keeping America's Promise: Challenges for Community College Leaders" (McClenney 2004):

- About two-thirds of community college students are part-time students
- 54 percent of community college students work full-time

- 34 percent of community college students have dependents and 16 percent are single parents
- More than 45 percent of community college students are first generation
- Almost 44 percent of community college students are 25 years or older

How does one implement SEM across several learner groups found at community colleges—not just academic for credit, but non-credit courses, adult education, and community learning? Open access at community colleges brings a diverse group of students to campuses with a wide range of educational needs and abilities. More adults, women, and first-generation students make up the community college population than that of four-year colleges. Students are more likely to take distance learning courses and desire non-traditional class times.

The diverse student population at community colleges affects SEM initiatives in numerous ways. Community colleges must create and market an institutional image that reaches out to all types of students and often limit their marketing efforts to specific service areas. In many cases admissions and marketing efforts are directed in smaller recruiting territories than four-year initiatives, resulting in the development of closer personal contacts with high school counselors, students, and parents. A SEM plan for recruiting students needs to focus on high school students, adult students, workforce development, and the needs of senior citizens.

Specialized Student Challenges

Once on campus, the varied types of students that attend community colleges bring with them a multitude of retention challenges. Finding ways to connect "drive-in" students to the campus constitutes a major issue facing community college enrollment managers. Many community college students attend classes part-time and work full-time. Additional challenges students face include:

- Finding a niche
- Knowing where to find assistance and having the ability to ask for help
- Competing allegiances such as family, friends, work, and non-college peers
- Balancing finances
- Longer completion time for degrees

- Lack of concrete goals
- The probability of being underprepared academically
- The probability of enrolling in at least one developmental class

Multiple Goals

Students at four-year institutions have one goal—graduation. At two-year institutions, the goals set by students may not even include the thought of graduation. A recent study showed that only 10 to 30 percent of first-time, full-time, degree-seeking students graduated from community colleges in three years (Bailey 2005). While many students ultimately want to graduate from community colleges, consider these other student goals:

- Taking a class, or classes solely for personal pleasure
- Attending college to upgrade skills, but not intending to graduate
- Attending college to fulfill work requirements
- Attending college to maximize the number of transfer credits to a four-year institution

With students having the ability to be "successful" without graduating, SEM managers must also have numerous goals tailored to the needs of multiple types of students. The resulting difficulty resides in finding ways to measure the success of the SEM plan. Simply defining the targeted areas can be difficult. What, exactly, is an at-risk student at a community college? How can an institution benchmark its data with other institutions?

CONCLUSION

This chapter began by suggesting that SEM offers a conceptual framework for meeting today's enrollment and financial challenges. The subsequent chapters in this book attempt to address these numerous and often new challenges currently confronting community colleges—and all institutions of higher education. In such a context, there are no easy solutions. However, it is the purpose of this book to provide guideposts for the way forward.

2

WHAT IS A SUCCESSFUL
Community College
Student?

by **Bruce Clemetsen** *and* **Jeff Rhodes**

2 For many stakeholders outside higher education with concerns about performance, the definition of student success is limited to how long a student remains enrolled and whether the student completes a degree. However, simply measuring student success in terms of a graduation rate is inappropriate because each institution across the nation serves a different population with differing needs, abilities, and levels of preparation (Swail, *et al.* 2008). The concept of student "swirling" has been well documented as a phenomenon that characterizes a significant segment of the community college population (De Los Santos and Wright 1990). While relatively easy to compile and understand, for many inside community colleges, these metrics are too narrow and reflect a lack of appreciation for the complexity of the community college mission and the transient nature of community college students. Fortunately efforts exist, supported in part by the notion of SEM, to capture more comprehensive measures of student success. The Lumina Foundation, in cooperation with the American Association of Community Colleges (AACC) and numerous other groups, established Achieving the Dream in 2004 with the mission to develop a long-term community college success agenda (Lincoln 2009). This is just one of a number of efforts to be discussed in this chapter.

Naturally the success of students determines a successful community college. But, who is a successful student, and what is a successful community college? The debate of this question is filled with diverse metrics and examples of effective programs that transcend the people involved. Strategic enrollment management utilizes data to guide decision making and design systems that support students and meet community college goals. Enrollment managers at community colleges possess the data and skills to lead the college towards enhanced student and institutional success. Employing a SEM perspective will connect data that demonstrates success to the goals and resource needs of the institution. The difficulty lies in determining what data to collect and interpret for the general public and policy makers. This effort is best undertaken using a general model that allows the institution to demonstrate its success while maintaining its uniqueness within the higher education landscape.

In contrast, uniform measures of success imposed by external agencies and governing boards typically fail to account for the wide variety of needs, goals, and levels of preparedness that exist within each new entering class. Furthermore, simple measures applied to all institutions fail to account for the unique needs of the population each institution is charged with serving. Even with a new president hailing the value of the workforce development mission of the community college, the general public often fails to grasp the broad mission of the community college and the difficulty in demonstrating achievement of that mission. Legislators insist upon accountability, evidenced by the plethora of performance-based funding initiatives constructed and impressed onto colleges. Yet, they measure performance simply by the number of degrees awarded. While recognizing the value of an associate's degree is progress, those who insist upon this unit of measure still fail to recognize that a degree, baccalaureate or associate, is in fact, the culmination of numerous smaller successes on the part of the student and the institution. Adelman (1999) found that graduation rates as a measure of success for an institution are largely meaningless in determining an institution's success in meeting the myriad needs of its population. The legislators who demand accountability have helped to create the broad spectrum of needs that the community college is tasked with meeting. The 2003 educational reauthorization committee meetings in Congress established accessibility as one of the guiding tenets of their legislation (King and Fox 2007). Accessibility carries with it the responsibility for helping students build skills in which they are deficient. This skill building occurs in the developmental programs at which community colleges excel, however, it is rarely recognized as a measure of success for either the student or the institution. The baccalaureate degree remains the penultimate measure of success for policy-makers who ignore the credentials and milestones earned along the way.

In order to demonstrate success, we must recognize the milestones and transitions that constitute every student's educational journey. For many first-generation students, walking into the admissions office at a local community college represents a major ordeal; therefore its completion should be recognized as a successful step toward accomplishing one's goals. For millions of students annually, filling out the FAFSA in hopes of acquiring the funding necessary to attend college is a success in and of itself. In addition, registration for courses involves the use of a complicated Web-based system that requires the student to acquire new technology aptitudes. Identification of clear goals and a path to their achievement is challenging enough, even more so when skill deficiencies create additional barriers to overcome. Successful completion of a single course requires sound teaching and significant effort from the student. Each of these smaller successes build toward achieving one's dreams. And, as such, it is incumbent upon those who shape the community college to adopt a broad perspective when defining student success.

Student success is a core element of any effort to incorporate strategic enrollment management (SEM) into the culture of a community or technical college. SEM offers a foundation for decision making that balances access, success, effectiveness, and efficiency. Bontrager (2004a) ties student success into a definition of enrollment management for community colleges: "Enrollment management is a complex set of concepts and processes that enables fulfillment of institutional mission and students' educational goals…" (p. 12). There are a growing number of initiatives in community colleges, such as the Achieving the Dream Initiative targeted at changing institutional cultures to focus on the success of students. SEM should not be seen as a competing perspective, but one that further informs and supports the growing interest in improving student success. SEM seeks to assist institutions in achieving mission-related goals by balancing resources to maximize student success.

Community colleges and technical colleges were designed for access (Cohen and Brawer 2003). Access has been seen as the hallmark of success for this uniquely American institution. Hence the wider the net could be cast into the community, the stronger the college's connection to those it was asked to serve and educate. From an enrollment management perspective, we operated from a "build it and they will come" approach. The success of the community college movement is a testament that "they came," and "they" keep coming. As a result, we now have more diversity of needs, abilities, experiences, cultures, goals, and dreams. With the movement to educational learning outcomes, accountability initiatives, and student consumerism, community and technical colleges face the directive to demonstrate their success beyond providing access to the postsecondary pipeline. Few understand why so many people come in our doors, but leave so soon without apparently having completed anything worth the money, time, and effort committed by students, taxpayers, and other financing entities. Community and technical college effectiveness is no longer understood merely in terms of access metrics; instead, we are called upon to prove educational effectiveness by defining and producing evidence of student success in terms of measurable outcomes. Community colleges are the most difficult institutional type to assess because they serve students with a wide array of goals, including transfer to a baccalaureate-granting institution, acquisition of vocational skills, development of basic skills, personal enrichment, or retooling for a new job or career (Basken 2008).

A growing obsession with the transfer component of the community college mission exists, fostering a myopic view of the educational purpose of two-year institutions. It is a widely held notion that any student who does not complete a baccalaureate degree has failed to achieve meaningful educational success, a notion forced upon community colleges in particular. This idea has been perpetuated, in part, by an outdated methodology at the Department of Education, which measures graduation rates by those who enter a baccalaureate-granting institution and complete that degree within six years (150 percent of the "normal" time frame for said degree). For more than half of the postsecondary students in the United States who attend community colleges, nothing could be further from the truth. Students often utilize community college opportunities to achieve shorter-term goals that lead to more immediate vocational, employment, and income results. Furthermore, although the "2+2" paradigm for community college students is viewed as the singular path to success, it is followed by a very small segment of the community college population. Whole forests have been felled to publish the research on transfer students, and that effort has made it clear that the transfer path from community colleges to universities is far from linear (De Los Santos and Wright 1990; Cejda 1999; Cejda and Kaylor 2001; Arnold 2001; Harbin 1997; Kearney 1995; Kintzer and Wattenbarger 1985; Mitchell and Grafton 1985; Palmer, Ludwig, and Stapleton 1994; Piland 1995; Porter, Hogan, and Gebel 2000). In addition, we have yet to determine what ethic, policy, or law holds that for a community college student to be successful she must transfer to a baccalaureate-granting institution. Cosand (1979, cited in Cohen and Brawer 2003) stated that evaluation for community colleges primarily rests on the success of their students in transferring to, and graduating from, four-year colleges and universities. The Educational Policy Institute stated that only one out of every three students at public community colleges complete a certificate or associate's degree within six years (Swail, *et al.* 2008). However, Adelman (2000) stated that, given the myriad reasons students give for utilizing the opportunities at community colleges, evaluation of "success" should focus on students achieving their personal goals, rather than on institutions achieving specific graduation or transfer rates. Adelman (1989) also found that the community college is an "intermediary institution" for students moving between enrollment and classification statuses, stating further that for some students, the community college is a "testing ground" to determine the viability of their postsecondary goals.

The multiple doors to the community college, along with the multiple entries and exits a community member may complete throughout any given time frame, make SEM efforts exceptionally challenging. Faculty and staff may only become aware of this aspect of the college when they want to improve tracking of their students in order to monitor outcomes. They soon come to realize the complexity of their simple request as it becomes apparent that the students in their programs might be simultaneously enrolled in multiple parts of the community college. Reviewing a program's student enrollments or pathways may reveal some students counted as being in other programs, and success may be different for each course and program in which the student is engaged at the time. They also realize that, for some students, the intensity of time in a program changed over the course of the academic year. This phenomenon epitomizes the "loosely coupled system" concept that Weick (1976) used to explain the organizational model of the postsecondary world. How do we develop an ability to manage this type of enrollment pattern, and how do we establish any measure of success that captures this level of complexity, which is not accidental, but intentional on the part of students?

DEFINING AND MEASURING STUDENT SUCCESS

How often have you been in a meeting where the topic of student success arises and the group quickly becomes engaged in a debate about what is meant by the phrase? The participants are typically all correct based on the lens they are applying and the reference point of how they work with students. Any institution that includes student success as a variable in an enrollment management plan must be ready for a rigorous debate that results in a multifaceted assessment. Enrollment managers may be helpful in recognizing the diversity, rather than divergence, of what colleagues view as success. However, for external stakeholders, the debate typically results in definitions and related variables that strip the concept of its inherent complexity, thereby reducing its ability to call all aspects of a community college to action in an aligned effort to support student success. However, efforts at institutional levels to determine what student success means and how to develop enrollment management plans and strategies to support the definition exist. There are also numerous efforts in various states to determine a definition of student success in relation to state accountability and performance measures. Reviewing some of these provides a rich sampling of the diversity of efforts that assist enrollment managers in shaping similar definitions and related metrics at their community colleges.

Models for Defining Success Metrics

Reviewing models of success can offer enrollment managers a structure to guide the organization of the multiple definitions and variables for determining student success. Some obvious examples of this concept follow; many that are more complex exist, but we also must keep our models as simple as possible to enable a broader understanding. We encourage enrollment managers to continually stay abreast of developing models and to seek out models that have been developed or successfully used at other community colleges.

Culver (2008) proposed a "student success funnel" to measure student success. This model measures persistence and progression rates for specific student populations each semester and year, providing more immediate feedback than the six-year graduation rate. A significant distinction between the two measures provides important success data. Persisters are those students who return for a subsequent semester or academic year. Progression rates are more specific and can be applied to completion of prerequisites, skill building, removal from academic probation, or completion of set percentages of a student's degree or another academic goal. The flexibility of this model allows an institution to serve the unique needs of each of its students while clearly demonstrating progress and institutional effectiveness.

Dietsche (2007, cited in Swail, *et al.* 2008) proposed a simple model that described four types of students according to their enrollment and academic standing. In that model, students' success is noted even if they choose to leave the institution (*see* Table 2.1). As stated earlier, typically, a student who leaves an institution, even in good academic standing, is seen as a failure on the part of the student and the institution unless that student leaves with a credential in his hand.

The primary strength of this model lies in its adherence to the mission of access. Private, selective institutions traditionally have much higher persistence, progression, and graduation rates simply because they only accept for admission those highly qualified, highly motivated students who face minimal barriers to success (Jaschik 2008). Conversely, community colleges, as mentioned earlier, were founded upon the mission of access, reaching out to students who face multiple barriers to success. Cejda (1999) found that three-fourths of students studied utilized the community college in an "occasional needs" role, enrolling for twelve or fewer hours on their way to the baccalaureate degree. The traditional definition of success (associate's degree within three years) would classify these students as dropouts, a failure on the part of the institution, when in fact the community college served exactly their needs at a specific point in time. The community college is also clearly successful in facilitating entry into the postsecondary pipeline for minorities, with the majority of minority first-time postsecondary enrollment occurring there (Provasnik and Planty 2008; Knapp, Kelly-Reid, and Ginder 2009).

TABLE 2.1. TYPES OF STUDENTS AT A POSTSECONDARY INSTITUTION BY ACADEMIC ACHIEVEMENT AND REGISTRATION STATUS [1]

Academic Achievement	Registration Status	
	Persist	Leave
PASS	Successful Persister	Successful Leaver
FAIL	Failed Persister	Failed Leaver

[1] (Dietsche 2007, cited in Swail, et al. 2008)

COMPREHENSIVE VIEWS OF STUDENT SUCCESS

Enrollment managers concerned about student success will direct efforts to explain the transitions experienced by students entering and exiting the myriad doors to the community college. Leading SEM efforts that enhance student success across the institution will require a diverse set of lenses that allow the enrollment manager to assist each individual student. Leaders must also establish general factors that can be efficiently and effectively applied across students and programs to articulate their goals of the institutional missions of access and success.

There are many transition points for students in community colleges; a non-exhaustive list might include:

- Adult basic skills to GED
- GED to credit
- English language learning to GED
- English language learning to credit
- Developmental studies to college level credit
- High school to college
- Workforce to credit
- Workforce to continuing education

Within these transitions students must make other adjustments in order to succeed. Understanding the nature of the transition requires knowledge of several factors, including the structure and outcomes of the program, how the program is taught, what engages students in the learning process, and the goals of the students in the program. Success is more likely when program delivery aligns with student ability and learning preferences and when program outcomes align with student goals and intent. Aligning the systems and programs with student variables and intent improves the probability of students achieving their educational goal.

With a SEM perspective, it is important to know which transitions are the most vital to institutional and community goals. Though we value all the opportunities our institutions provide, some opportunities are vital to the stability of the institution. It is not feasible in an environment of continuous fiscal constraint to make adjustments and investments in all the areas impacting student success. Some critical questions to consider are:

● What student markets could be expanded with improved success?
● What transitions have the greatest cost to replace students who depart early?
● What students and related transitions are most closely tied to the institutional mission?
● Which programs have low cost, high demand, and available capacity?
● Which programs have students making successful transitions resulting in high progress and persistence rates?

Addressing these and other related questions focus SEM efforts to improve student success.

Adelman (2007b) has called on community colleges to develop a "culture of transfer." This concept targets improved preparation and flow of students between K–12, the community college, and baccalaureate institutions. The ethos of a "culture of transfer" provides a powerful lens from which to view SEM in community colleges. Though our focus here is broader than the path to the baccalaureate, the essential elements present in a "culture of transfer" are worth noting and reflecting upon in relation to the various transitions, or transfers, a student may experience with the community college. Necessary elements for the existence of a "culture of transfer" are:

● On-going reflection of the systems
● Groups and tracking that influence the curriculum among the programs a student may transfer between
● Data and information that bring to light student progress and direct interventions in the system
● Assessment of students
● Language that keeps student progress at the forefront of conversations

Establishing a "culture of transfer" supports the traditional role of community colleges, while also providing a method for bringing focus to student progress between educational programs at a community college.

Bontrager (2004b) has shared a model he refers to as the student success continuum. Figure 2.1 (on page 22) represents the traditional enrollment perspective still prevalent among many in higher education. This model displays a classical silo approach to SEM. Enrollment management professionals may be aware of the other institutional elements impacting student success, however, little coordinated effort exists.

In contrast, Bontrager (2004b) believes SEM efforts must move from being overly focused on organizational structure to being attentive to students and their transitions, developing into an approach more aligned with the student success continuum (Figure 2.2, on page 23). The student success continuum model offers insight about a system of transitions between institutional components impacting SEM efforts targeted at student success.

The Research and Planning Group for California Community Colleges conducted a qualitative study on two-to-four year transfer practices (Serban 2008). Though the project focused on traditional two-year to four-year transfer, some of the categories of successful transfer practices translate to a culture of transition that supports student success across the many dimensions of a community college. Four of the six transfer supporting factors provide useful information regarding the

FIGURE 2.1 ▶

Traditional Silo Approach to Enrollment

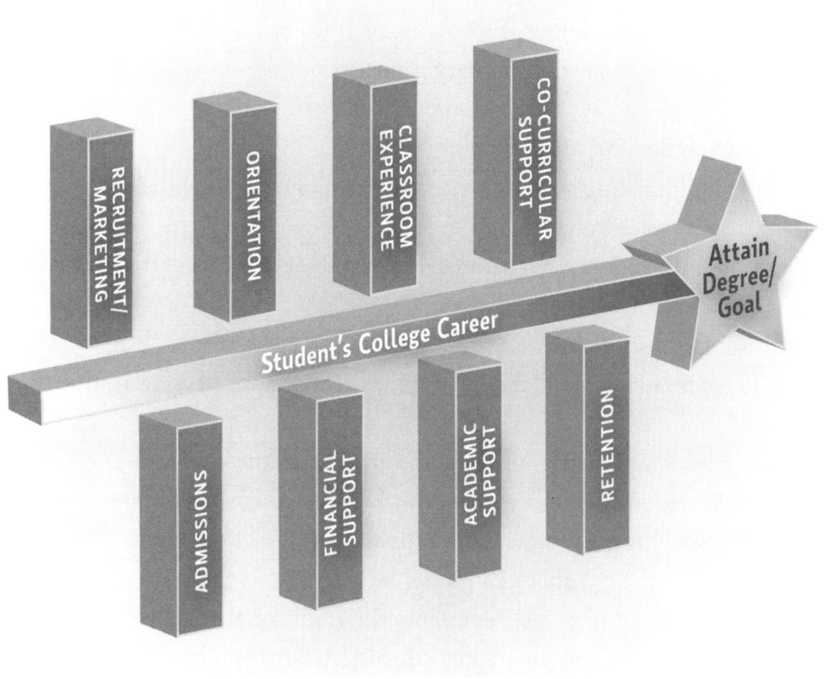

creation of a student success oriented SEM program: 1) evidence of a supportive culture; 2) an institutional climate that is student focused; 3) relationships among organizations that work together to support student success; and 4) financial aid support services (Serban 2008).

First, the marked presence of a culture that supports student progress is vital for promoting student success (Kinzie and Kuh 2007). The community college has visible symbols and events that celebrate student milestones (*e.g.*, scholarship award ceremonies, honor society inductions, commencement.) The relationship between content and other courses, as well as the world beyond the classroom make transparent the purpose and value of the curriculum and co-curriculum (Pascarella and Terenzini 1991). Additionally clear course and program outcomes that highlight the alignment of curriculum and co-curricular support enable students to see progress that leads to success.

The second factor from the California study (Serban 2008) that gives clarity to SEM efforts is a call for an environment tailored to students and their success. The

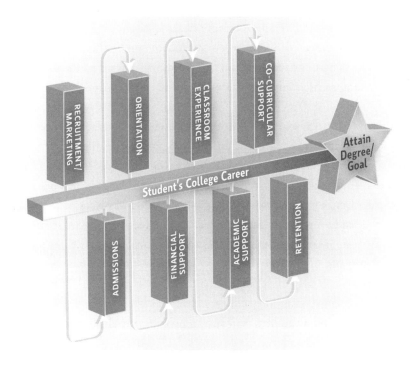

◄ **FIGURE 2.2**

Student Success
Approach to SEM

research identified several support programs that fill the prescription for a student success environment:

- Peer role models of success
- Integrated academic support services
- Early warning systems
- Assessment that supports "meeting students where they are"
- Communication that highlights the value and belief in each student to succeed
- Strategic demographic program development
- High touch—strategic use of technology that engages faculty and staff in assisting students

While not new programs or concepts, growing amounts of research support their value in the endeavor to enhance student success. SEM professionals in community colleges should be reviewing the efficacy of implementation on their own campus (Serban 2008).

Third, strategic external relationships are vital to student success. The community college must know its feeders and receivers. As obvious as this may sound, it can prove difficult. Where cooperation and collaboration focused on the success of students are present, rather than institutional politics, program and pathway development, academic and skill preparation, and articulation are likely to support success. The California study (Serban 2008) notes the valuable role of accurate articulation with a process that engages faculty. Articulation agreements between community colleges and employers are just as valuable in promoting student success as those between two and four-year institutions. Whether a student transfers her skills to a baccalaureate program or the workforce, goals are met and success is reached.

Lastly, the study highlights financial aid as an effective support service for assisting with student transfer. It is valuable for SEM professionals to implement financial aid preparation and processing as early in the student pipeline as possible. The study focuses on beginning financial aid in early high school. While certainly very beneficial, many community colleges have seen merit in beginning the financial aid education and awareness program in middle schools. Regardless, financial aid awareness and preparation assistance is very important to supporting student success (Serban 2008).

The influence of institutional commitment constitutes an interesting factor related to campus climate. Viewing faculty and staff indicators of this factor, the study assesses the process of establishing campus reputations. Interestingly, an environment supportive of student success exists when employees create an ethos and reward structure where institutional reputations and success are based on student achievements. SEM professionals typically know who these people are, but we need to highlight their value and formal or informal leadership in promoting critical factors that support student success (Serban 2008).

Measuring Student Success

In the inaugural volume of the *Enrollment Management Journal*, Ryan (2007) suggested a framework of four research principles for enrollment managers to use in supporting student success: 1) research that provides data on systemic issues; 2) an integration of various research schools of thought; 3) establishing clear terminology and scalable definitions; and 4) use of multiple methodologies and designs. Accommodating the multiple definitions that can exist within a campus requires a diverse approach to measuring student success. As interest in accountability increases, the diversity of campus definitions shape state level measures. Though numerous campus efforts to define and measure student success on community college campuses exist, viewing those that have risen to the state level offers enrollment managers a better view on how to develop campus-based SEM practices and assessment. Examples of how various states engage in attempting to capture and utilize broad measures of success that can be used to support SEM at community colleges follow.

Sanchez and Laanan (1997) examined 841,000 community college completers and leavers in California from the 1991–92 academic year and found that all students experienced increases in earnings one, two, and three years after completing their studies. These students included those in non-credit vocational programs, those with credit hours completed but no degree, and those who completed the associate's degree. Their work makes it clear that students benefit from even the smallest successes in their enrollment.

The Texas Higher Education Coordinating Board allows its community colleges to report as successes those students who have completed all or specific portions of the statewide core curriculum (for transfer), along with those who complete vocational certificates and associate's degrees. Furthermore, Texas recognizes what is called a "Marketable Skills Achievement" award, which consists of nine to fourteen semester credit hours or 144 to 359 non-credit clock hours of instruction (THECB Educational Data Center 2007).

The University of Alaska at Anchorage (which awards associate's and baccalaureate degrees) chose to track each student's success with five questions:

- Did you return the next year?
- Did you transfer?
- Did you graduate with a degree?
- Did you graduate with an interim degree (short of your eventual goal)?
- Are you achieving grades that qualify as a success to stay on track to earning a degree?

(Jaschik 2008)

In Virginia, a course-based model of measuring success was developed and used to demonstrate the success of Thomas Nelson Community College (TNCC). Quanty, Dixon, and Ridley (1996) found that students transferring from TNCC to Christopher Newport University (CNU) performed well in prerequisite courses. They measured students' performance in upper-division courses after completing prerequisites at either TNCC or CNU. The community college transfer students performed at a level equivalent to the native CNU students after a re-sequencing of course content to facilitate continuity in usage of learned skills. As such, the success of the community college in preparing students for transfer was well documented.

A new set of accountability measures have emerged for community colleges in Maryland. As described by Keller (2007b), the new measures focus on evaluating community colleges on value-added features of "successful persistence." The goal of the new indicators is to capture the achievements of community college students that did not intend to transfer or complete a degree. Students are categorized according to college readiness indicators that determine student persistence. This approach accommodates a broader definition of student success and accounts for the wide range of student educational readiness. Furthermore it holds to the basic fact that not all students intend to achieve a degree or transfer within a three or six-year time frame.

One project based on a model of "Milestone Events" developed by Ewell (2007) has gained wide recognition for addressing the complex nature of defining student success is being undertaken by the Washington State Board for Community and Technical Colleges. In a 2008 Community College Research Center report "Using Longitudinal Data to Increase Community College Student Success: A Guide to Measuring Milestone and Momentum Point Attainment," authors Leinbach and Jenkins report on the development and use of milestones and momentum points for measuring student progress. Milestones comprise measurable achievements, encompassing the most common measures of completion and intermediate outcomes. Momentum points consist of measurable attainments correlated to milestones. Compiling student data to view longitudinal student enrollment patterns and achievement generates a rich resource for developing programs and allocating resources to promote student success. Leinbach and Jenkins state that, "Understanding how students actually progress through their college programs is essential in developing strategies and choosing appropriate interventions to improve student outcomes" (2008, p. 1) This assessment model and correlated definition of student success provides a solid foundation for any enrollment management team to have a broad impact on visible institutional success.

For SEM professionals in community and technical colleges, several elements of the model make it a powerful tool for defining and assessing student success.

- Milestones and momentum points can be identified for the continuum of academic programs at a community or technical college, inviting the involvement of all academic units and faculty in improving student success.
- Critical points of continued academic progress are identified for additional study, focusing on effective teaching and support services to enhance student progress.
- Interventions can be made through a prevention orientation as a result of knowing where students will experience significant challenge.

For an enrollment manager or team to see the full spectrum of student success allows for SEM to diffuse throughout the community or technical college.

...hin Oregon, there is an intense effort to define student success in order to ...blish fair and accurate accountability metrics, as well as to also establish ongo- ...g understanding about student behavior and resource allocation to support student achievement. The result of these efforts in Oregon is to provide a context for stakeholders to understand student success in the multiple contexts of students at the state's comprehensive community colleges. The community colleges will also gain in knowledge about student progress and achievement in order to improve institutional effectiveness.

Community colleges in Oregon have joined efforts to use the Washington model and added elements to support a more strategic enrollment management effort across the state. To advance a statewide student success initiative, Oregon community colleges are analyzing statewide data to determine student progress milestones and momentum points. There is a simultaneous effort to collect and compile institutional best practices that explain the milestone and momentum point findings. The value of this combined effort recognizes a broad definition of student success and gives enrollment managers information to facilitate effective collaboration across the state. This effort will accommodate students who move between institutions and replicate efforts that result in enhanced success for target populations. Furthermore, this effort provides the impetus for state resources to fund effective statewide efforts that support student success.

These initiatives provide enrollment managers in community colleges with data and a model for student success that reflects the many transition points a person may make as a lifelong learner at their local community or technical college. Successful enrollment management strategies assist students in their transitions to new educational aspirations and contexts. Strategic enrollment management at community colleges requires close attention to the transitions a community member must complete in order to fulfill his academic goals.

ADVISING AS THE KEYSTONE TO STUDENT SUCCESS

Effective advising represents the key to establishing student-specific success measures and demonstrating that our institutions facilitate this success. In the same vein, the means to demonstrating community college effectiveness is the collection of data on student goals. This data collection constitutes part of the advising process, thus advisors become advocates for the institution in the same way that they advocate for students. The model presented here holds that the advising function is a significant part of the co-instructional education that students receive outside the classroom (Pascarella and Terenzini 1991). Far more than assistance with course selection, advising must be viewed as a process that continues throughout a student's educational career. A student-centered relationship with two-way interaction, shared initiative, high trust, collaborative assessment of progress, and sincere belief in the student's potential characterizes effective advising (Habley and Bloom 2007). Whether an institution utilizes full-time advisors or relies solely on advisors from the faculty, their effectiveness outside the classroom will translate into comparable results in student achievement, measured and confirmed through the data collected and analyzed throughout each student's academic career.

Figure 2.3 (on page 30) demonstrates the cyclical nature of the student/advisor relationship and the process used to measure students' goals and related institutional performance. When the number of successful students increases, the effectiveness of the institution is made clear to internal and external stakeholders and policy makers. Current database systems in use at colleges across the country are more than capable of being adjusted to allow for data on incremental goals to be entered and the outcomes posted. Many institutions require that students meet with an advisor prior to registering for an upcoming semester. It is in this advising session, which is in itself an instructional event (Habley and Bloom 2007; Pascarella and Terenzini 1991), that goals are defined, reviewed, and assessed and the necessary data can be collected. In addition, completion of these goals is noted in the database for reporting purposes, and updated goals are posted. The student's updated goals guide course selection and further assessment of long-term goals. The short-term goals of skill building and unit course completion lead to completion of longer-term goals of program completion and transfer or entrance into the workforce. At each step, both the student and the institution can recognize and celebrate successes that demonstrate achievement of mission. Each transition or transfer a student embarks upon begins the cycle anew, an occasion for the assessment and establishment of a fresh slate of goals. Furthermore, this model empowers students to critically assess their own ambitions and the method for achievement. Community colleges no longer play the role of "cooling out" students' ambitions (Cohen and Brawer 2003), and advising is no longer simply a review of the academic catalog and courses within a program, but an educational process and means of developing the lifelong learner.

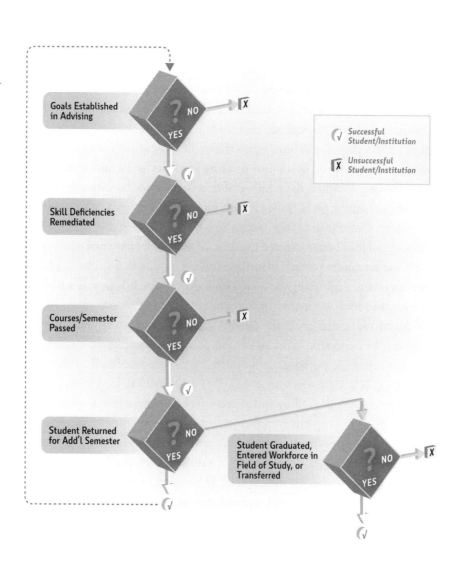

FIGURE 2.3 ▶

Rhodes' Model
for Assessment
of Student and
Institutional Success
through Advising

CONCLUSION

The debate about what constitutes a successful community college student will continue on campuses, in communities, and among policy makers. As an enrollment manager, you can play a role in shaping the conversation and adding breadth to the definitions discussed. Based on an individual's perspective concerning the role of the institution and their beliefs and values related to the business of teaching and learning, certain students and their success may appear to have more value in defining the success of the community college. Enrollment managers are sensitive to the diversity of definitions for student success at the student and administrative levels. We must also be ever mindful of how defining success influences the strategy of optimizing enrollments and resources. As advocates both for students and our institutions we must be prepared to defend the priorities of students' needs while protecting institutional viability.

A number of frameworks and models exist which can be used in working with others to develop a definition. The myriad voices of students who want to be acknowledged for their success, and the voices of those who are dedicated to teaching these students must comprise a crucial component for consideration. For the enrollment manager, developing a model of current and ideal processes, informed by students and stakeholders, is important work that guides planning, assessment, and resource allocation, ultimately defining the community college's success at meeting the changing needs of the community and its citizens.

This chapter highlights a few state efforts to define and measure student success. These undertakings reflect diverse approaches to communicating the quantitative story of student success across the broad range of expectations people have for the variety of educational opportunities available at community colleges. Encouragingly there is clear evidence that some states are accepting a definition of student success that is not overly simplified as degrees and graduation rate, but far more representative of the diversity of our students and the multiple missions of community colleges. The broader definitions and related metrics mentioned in this chapter provide excellent models for guiding strategic efforts to improve and sustain student success.

It is vital to focus and connect SEM efforts to student success in community colleges. Presently, federal legislation calling for improved effectiveness of community colleges is being written, based on the traditional and over-simplified definitions already shown as inadequate. Those community colleges able to infuse SEM perspectives and practices into discussions of institutional strategy and effectiveness will be most prepared to meet these challenges and demonstrate their success in meeting students' needs on an individual and community basis. As SEM is practiced on campus, and the institution better understands its students, itself, and the interaction between the two, the community college develops a culture with the capacity to change and make continuous improvements for the sake of student success.

3

STRATEGIC ENROLLMENT MANAGEMENT AND
Instructional Division

by **Bruce Clemetsen**

3 Strategic enrollment management is necessarily comprehensive in its application to a community college and, therefore, must be inclusive of a college's instructional division. As Kerlin (2008) posits in her definition of SEM for community colleges, any effort must be coordinated and support the multiple missions of the college. We realize the multiple missions of the institution most plainly by looking at the various academic units at a community college. Kerlin's definition reminds us of the imperative to connect SEM to the institution's strategic plan, as well as to the academic master plan for guidance in shaping future enrollments and balance necessary revenues with program expansion. SEM facilitates educational achievement by effectively connecting educational program opportunities with students who have congruent learning goals.

CONNECTING SEM TO THE INSTITUTIONAL CORE OF TEACHING AND LEARNING

To be comprehensive, SEM in the community college must reinforce the missions of the institution. Bob Bontrager stresses the mission driven nature of SEM. He explains, "This involves understanding the unique role an institution plays in the environment it operates in and how to translate that role into attracting and retaining students" (2004a, p. 12). Community college missions generally reflect the needs of the communities they were founded to serve, as they have been typically grounded in meeting the educational needs of local areas. Bontrager goes on to note, "An institution cannot be all things to all people" (p. 12). Herein lies the challenge of SEM from a community college perspective; community colleges, through their longstanding focus on access, serve virtually all aspects of a community, the epitome of an organization determined to be all things to all people. Even a cursory review of academic programs reveals a highly diverse organization, creating great challenges for the SEM professional.

The meshing of SEM with a community college's academic master plan moves enrollment management into a core planning process for instructional units. The League of Innovation (2009) defines the academic master plan as:

- An academic master plan (Learning Plan) provides a framework for decision making and resource allocation in the instructional areas of the college.
- The academic master plan allows other units of the college to develop plans that support achievement of the Learning Plan.
- The academic master plan supports teaching and learning.
- The academic master plan is a "30,000 foot level" look that provides future directions and goals for the institution.

The Society for College and University Planning (2009) provides additional information in its definition of academic master planning that illuminates the connection to SEM:

Other planners on a campus rely on the information and plans that they receive from academic planners to know what buildings to upgrade, what student services are necessary, what books and journals to acquire, and what technology to support (p. 1).

Clearly, the institution benefits greatly by utilizing SEM as part of the implementation of an academic master plan.

Calls from long-time leaders in the SEM movement have routinely identified the need for enrollment managers to be conscientious of their relationship with instruction. Dolence (1993) suggested that the interaction between the academic components of the institution, including curriculum and policy, and students' decisions about matriculating, persisting, and departing guide recruitment and retention efforts of the institution. Bontrager contends that the ultimate success of a SEM initiative depends on the degree of connectivity with the academic enterprise.

Additionally, "effective enrollment managers take every opportunity to support and promote the academic program" (2004a, p. 12). Stan Henderson (2005) cautions us that SEM has been overly focused on organizational structures, highlighting the need to re-engage our understanding of the academic enterprise. This preoccupation with structure has tended to create SEM silos that have little direct contact with faculty (Smith 2008). By entering into this conversation, SEM managers and structures can be better integrated into the institutional mission.

Common linkages exist between SEM and instructional goals. As stated above, an academic master plan reveals the direction and future needs of the academic enterprise to ensure the redesign of systems and services to effectively and efficiently support teaching and learning. Bontrager (2004a) offers several reasons for a connection to the academic enterprise that apply equally to community colleges: promoting academic quality, connecting faculty with students, maintaining program vitality as measured by enrollment and demand, and developing program specific efforts as career options and market demands shift. Making connections to faculty around these issues results in the necessary broad institutional effort to enhance student access and success, develop innovative partnerships with diverse constituents, and produce value in the local community.

Community colleges that have successfully embraced SEM beyond enrollment services have found ways to integrate SEM concepts into the creation and nurturing of faculty relationships. Clayton Smith notes that more enrollment managers are concentrating on viewing SEM from an academic framework, realizing that, "to have effective SEM operations, [SEM professionals] must place SEM within the institutional academic context" (2008, p. 2). This focus supports what Henderson described as an "enrollment management ethos" (2005, p. 5). Creating this SEM ethos requires SEM professionals to lead efforts that clearly involve and support faculty in meeting mutual goals for the benefit of students and the institution. Developing these relationships and maintaining SEM's relevance to instructional units never stops given that SEM constitutes a continuous process of supporting student and institutional success.

There are guides for pursuing the connection with instruction. Guides for discussion include the research instruments of the Center for Community College Student Engagement (CCSSE), specifically the CCSSE benchmarks and SENSE design principles, and David Kalsbeek's *Four Orientations to Enrollment Management* (2006). These guides bring visibility to where relationships and connections with instruction can be established as part of a SEM effort.

CCSSE AND SENSE: FOUNDATIONS FOR ENGAGING FACULTY IN SEM

SEM efforts involving instructional units must be informed by a robust assessment plan. Adelman (2000) cautioned higher education about focusing on completion of credentials as the measure of success for community college students and as the measure of effectiveness for community colleges. He has called for a focus on students' progress and goal attainment as representing the more informative outcomes related to student success and institutional effectiveness. A discussion of student success is provided in chapter 2 of this book, but in the context of SEM in an instructional unit, this perspective gives credence to how enrollment and instructional leaders can assess and define collaborative efforts to maximize student success and institutional goals.

Assessment that involves and informs instructional units on factors that concern SEM professionals is supported by the work of the Center for Community College Student Engagement, and specifically the Community College Survey of Student Engagement (CCSSE) and the Survey of Entering Student Engagement (SENSE). These instruments and resulting reports provide guidance to instructional and SEM leadership about effective service and faculty efforts to promote student success. The reports are a catalyst for designing, assessing, and redesigning systematic approaches for an institution to improve student success.

Enrollment managers know the value of student involvement and engagement with learning impacts retention, progress, and educational goal attainment. The CCSSE provides a good measure of how much of this kind of engagement occurs in the classroom and across the community college. Instructional leaders and enrollment managers gain from CCSSE data to describe the success and failure of the institutional learning environment for maximizing student persistence, learning, and goal attainment. The 2006 report of CCSSE findings summarizes the importance of assessing student engagement,

Research shows that the more actively engaged students are—with college faculty and staff, with other students, and with the subject matter they study—the more likely they are to learn, to stick with their studies, and to attain their academic goals. Student engagement, therefore, is a valuable yardstick for assessing the quality of colleges' educational practices and identifying ways they can produce more successful results (p. 4).

This is hopefully not a new concept. Enrollment managers know the value of a student's connection to faculty and course content. Instruments such as CCSSE provide the data and benchmarking to support SEM, along with a strong foundation for working with instructional units to improve efforts to meet institutional SEM targets.

The five CCSSE benchmarks offer a collection of different conversations and planning opportunities for instructional units to employ in the fulfillment of a SEM plan:

- Active and collaborative learning
- Student effort
- Academic challenge
- Student-faculty interaction
- Support for learners

By simply reviewing the benchmarks, it is obvious that the engagement being assessed by CCSSE is that of the instructional environment most influenced by the faculty and instructional leadership. Hence, CCSSE can be an extremely useful tool for a SEM initiative targeted at the involvement of the instructional unit.

The infusion of data and information from CCSSE into SEM related conversations and efforts with instructional units have the potential to generate rich learning, stronger relationships, and new efforts to enhance the learning experience of students. Efforts surrounding assessment of learning outcomes have encountered various degrees of acceptance; there will always be those who punch holes in the methodology, psychometrics of the instrument, or scoff at the idea that anyone dare offer advice on how to improve teaching based on a survey. However, for those committed to improving teaching and learning, the data leads to enriching conversations among colleagues about how they teach, thus establishing common ground in faculty efforts. The resulting relationships from conversations about teaching and the five CCSSE benchmarks can generate ideas and energy to change pedagogy or at least try some new approaches in teaching. Support from instructional leaders and enrollment managers is critical to this process. Involving resources on campus that support faculty professional development helps to transition faculty to a more student-focused approach to teaching. Opportunity also exists to recognize those faculty members who already apply classroom practices that engage students at high levels. Numerous teaching practices, many to be found as best practices on the CCSSE Web site, can be instituted to impact student engagement.

Another instrument from the Center for Community College Student Engagement that informs both student services and instruction is the Survey of Entering Student Engagement. This instrument provides an assessment of what students experience as they enter the community college from early contact as a prospective student through the first few weeks of being in the classroom. The six design principles connect SEM to the work of the instructional unit. Using SENSE or similar instruments provides data that ties non-instructional support services to the classroom experience, focusing efforts of faculty and instructional leaders on how to influence SEM goals for retention and student success at the earliest point of students' educational experience at the community college.

Faculty has a direct and significant influence on a student's early experiences at the community college. The data collected by SENSE may aid in shaping the nature of the learning environment and the experiences of first-time students. The types of efforts based on the SENSE design principles undertaken by instructional units to support student success vary widely. The following simply provides an example of work connected to each principle from an academic orientation to SEM.

⬤ **PERSONAL CONNECTIONS.** Relationships are important, and assisting students in identifying a person or persons they know is committed to their success improves the likelihood of that success. Certainly many ways exist to design a classroom experience so that faculty have the opportunity to learn their students' names, goals, and motivation for taking the course. Community colleges like to point out that their smaller class sizes and strong commitment to teaching places students and faculty into a more intimate learning relationship than the one new students encounter at a university. Instructional and SEM leaders ought to find ways to leverage these competitive advantages to facilitate faculty actions that support this principle.

HIGH EXPECTATIONS AND ASPIRATIONS. Providing clear information about the community college's high expectations for performance and engagement and acknowledging students' high aspirations for their personal success creates common ground for the relationship between the student and the institution. Students attend college to achieve a goal that they believe will improve and enrich their lives. They have high expectations for themselves and for the college experience. The community college needs to unequivocally articulate expectations of students that will support individuals in reaching their educational goal.

Many new students enter the community college completely unaware of the expectations of the faculty and institution. Institutional rules abound and are often emphasized at the outset, but typically, little time is invested in explaining expectations. Faculty are critical in developing the expectations of students and playing a role in reinforcing them, thereby shaping the learning culture on the campus.

A PLAN AND A PATHWAY TO SUCCESS. Having a goal is important, therefore, guiding students towards establishing a goal, a plan to achieve that goal, and a system of regularly reviewing their progress produces an engaged learner. Setting and clearly communicating expectations about the paths to success support students in developing a plan to achieve their goals. The foundation of the advising system of the community college rests upon this principle. Clearly, faculty have concerns about student success and know the value of completing diplomas, certificates, or degrees. However, with the many access points, broad array of educational programs, and diverse student populations, the community college may face challenges when connecting students with an advisor or planning tools. Faculty involvement with student advising early in the student's experience is vital to SEM efforts. Additionally, visible, accessible, and easy to use academic planning tools (degree audits, articulation tables, transfer guides, program worksheets) comprise critical supporting resources for the advising system.

AN EFFECTIVE TRACK TO COLLEGE READINESS. Underprepared students persist more often when they have a clear understanding of the path and skill levels required to become college ready. This principle involves reviewing the placement of students and the methods in place for assisting them with completing developmental course work. This information, if not already collected and utilized by the institution, provides excellent material for understanding how to improve student skill development and performance in later college level courses. Faculty involvement in establishing and reviewing student placement is essential for supporting student success.

ENGAGED LEARNING. The evidence of student engagement emerges when curricular and co-curricular learning is intentional and pervasive throughout the early student experience. Students need to believe in the value of the classroom experience, and that they and others have the opportunity to integrate their own experiences with the learning process. The same concepts that impact the CCSSE student engagement benchmarks influence this principle. Building relationships among students through the learning of course content provides a student with a sense of competence and confidence. Instructional leaders and enrollment managers become better able to structure early academic experiences that foster second term or semester retention, influence the quality of the learning environment, and enhance student performance in entry-level developmental and college-level courses.

AN INTEGRATED NETWORK OF FINANCIAL, SOCIAL, AND ACADEMIC SUPPORT. Connecting students to resources and counselors who in turn connect students to services that support their chances for success improves engagement and persistence. SEM professionals understand the necessity of financial aid, co-curricular programs, and academic support services as part of a SEM initiative. Faculty, through advising, can play an important role in keeping students informed about important financial aid requirements and scholarship opportunities. Supporting faculty involvement in creating and advising student activities and organizations that facilitate learning beyond the classroom is a natural component of an academic SEM orientation. Faculty must possess a clear comprehension of academic support services (*i.e.*, tutoring, supplemental instruction, library services, technological support) in order to make accurate referrals and provide the correct guidance to students. The administration of the SENSE survey provides a learning opportunity for the participating community college. Because the survey focuses on new students, the process of identifying the sample of courses for participation in the survey provides information that reinforces the inclusion of instruction in SEM. The sampling of courses containing a large percentage of first-time students reveals the faculty with the most influence on student success behaviors and first to second term retention. Identification of this special group of faculty allows professional development to focus on implementing pedagogical practices that assist a new student's transition into college-level work, while establishing a relationship with a faculty member who can guide them to critical resources. The assessment of a student's entry-to-college experience provides the type of systemic view of a process critical for SEM efforts. Developing this type of view facilitates congruence between what the student experiences and learns about college before the classroom and what actually occurs in the early weeks of the semester or term. This allows for faculty involvement in the alignment of marketing, recruitment, placement, admissions, orientation, and initial advising, in the interest of influencing the student culture as it prepares to enter the classroom. Given our open door, systemically shaping expectations based on realities of the classroom fosters early and lasting student success.

The assessment of the full entry process connects various services with the classroom experience. Developing a data driven view of the entire entry and early academic experience sets forth the possibility for synergies between service and instruction. The SENSE survey provides information about student academic behaviors after having attended class for only a few weeks. Institutional leaders learn what habits students develop that impact their success in their first terms. While not an early warning system, this data provides a view of how well a community college teaches incoming students the expected behaviors required for success. Assessing the level of student-reported academic behavior provides an opportunity to review how well students are informed about academic expectations before they arrive at the classroom door. Enrollment and instructional leaders have an opportunity to concentrate on how to educate students about expected academic behavior, instead of simply on how to have enough students.

AN ACADEMIC ORIENTATION TO SEM

David Kalsbeek (2006a) posited the concept of an academic orientation to SEM structure and strategy.

> *An academic orientation to [SEM] focuses attention primarily on the development and integrity of academic programs, on the primacy of teaching and learning, recognizing that the development and delivery of academic curricula is higher education's core enterprise"* (p. 7).

The resulting strategy of this orientation centers on the creation and delivery of competitive curriculum in existing programs and the development of new programs. Academic programs must be developed for clearly identified community, university, and business needs. Identifying enrollment mix early as part of the curriculum design is crucial to ensure that sufficient students with optimum experience and abilities exist to fill the program. Simultaneously, delivery systems must align with the intended student market in order to support access, while maximizing success and goal achievement of students and the academic program.

The academic orientation to SEM has a number of strengths as a result of the intentional focus on relationships with faculty and instructional goals. These include:

- The focus of SEM on core academic purposes
- Integration of processes to maximize teaching and learning
- SEM at the core of institutional decision making
- SEM strategy guiding program development and evaluation (Kalsbeek, 2006a)

This orientation requires that faculty and instructional managers see SEM as enhancing program development and success, and not as a competing model or a structural impediment to the academic goals of the institution.

The academic orientation of SEM does contain weaknesses. Kalsbeek (2006a) acknowledged its susceptibility to developing too narrow a focus for recognizing relevant issues for markets, students, or systems. A strong faculty culture with workload and other fiscal stresses may result in a pulling back of support. Frustration over student performance and class size can result in turning the focus away from students' needs to faculty needs. Any retrenchment of faculty from SEM efforts leaves SEM in a silo; the scenario a faculty orientation helps to mitigate.

A SEM effort shaped by an academic framework would alter structural components of the means to pursue SEM. Kalsbeek (2006a) identifies four structural components utilized to support the academic orientation: academic support, academic transition, academic program development, and co-curricular and curricular integration. Each component involves various student services and instructional support departments. The structure focuses these services on critical issues regarding the support of students as learners and maximizing the creation of an environment focused on learning. Community college faculty and services tend to concentrate on supporting student success through strong academic skill development, student transition efforts that support incoming students and those re-entering the workforce upon completion of an educational goal, and the active facilitation of co-curricular activities that enhance the classroom experience.

The connection to academic program development represents an area for community college enrollment managers to engage more in the application of SEM. Here SEM leadership must be involved in the creation and implementation of the academic master plan, along with the early phases of program creation. New programs need a strategy for finding students and sustaining enrollment in order to ensure their ability to meet business and industry needs or to supply transfer students to upper division courses at universities. Infusing SEM concepts into the program development process assists faculty in considering various external and internal factors influencing program success—defined as sufficient enrollments. Providing faculty with environmental scan data concerning competition, economic development, and demographic trends informs the creation phase of new programs.

A SEM support team can facilitate this process. Such a group assists an instructional unit to "get the program off the ground." The team helps with market identification, advertising, and identification of feeder programs and partners. The ability to target scholarship dollars for an emerging program to attract students further entices instructional units to work with campus SEM experts.

Community colleges connect their strong commitment to teaching and learning with SEM through a structure focused on supporting student learning. The academic orientation provides a lens to view SEM as serving successful instruction and successful students.

INSTRUCTIONAL INVOLVEMENT IN SEM SYSTEMS

A structure that supports an academic orientation to SEM generates a number of opportunities for instructional leaders and faculty to engage students in facilitating a culture of learning. If instructional planning is supported by integration with SEM. then instructional units will more likely involve themselves in the work of enrollment management. A list of activities and services that provide points of collaboration and involvement on the part of faculty and between instructional and SEM leaders follows. While not intended to be comprehensive and not inclusive of information mentioned or implied in the preceding sections, it hopefully presents a myriad of opportunities for implementation of an academic orientation to SEM.

Recruitment

Instructional units typically understand the connection between student enrollment, FTE, and program viability. However, many faculty members do not see recruitment as their responsibility as teaching represents their primary commitment. However, some instructional departments may be very interested in recruitment work. To determine interest, an enrollment manager should review the structure and externally driven expectations of the program. Cohort programs and one-year certificate programs require a new group of students on a regular basis to survive. Faculty members in these programs are probably already active recruiters and can benefit from added support from enrollment service units. Programs that serve state or regional needs require more effort to ensure a continuous flow of enrollments and also benefit from a collaborative effort between faculty and enrollment services. Instructional programs supported with Carl Perkins funds demonstrate how working with enrollment services in recruiting efforts can assist with meeting benchmarks. Unfortunately, many instructional departments bring groups of high school students or community members to campus for a demonstration or workshop, while the faculty members maintain their teaching focus, not realizing their participation in a potentially powerful recruitment event. Enrollment managers can find many ways to involve faculty in recruitment, and may be astonished by the number of faculty likely involved in their own recruiting.

Admission Standards for Limited Enrollment Programs

For many allied health programs and other specialty trades, admission is competitive, meaning students must meet a variety of prerequisites in order to pursue courses for the certificate or degree. Faculty from these programs have significant interest in retaining students—seeing them complete the program successfully, and in select instances, becoming certified or licensed professionals. The establishment and evaluation of admission criteria necessarily involves the active participation of faculty. Enrollment managers assist with establishing student friendly processes to assess program readiness. They also encourage and provide support for the active assessment to validate admission requirements. Management of these programs requires a collaborative effort between instruction and enrollment services.

Scholarships

Faculty involvement in the awarding of scholarships allows instructional units to influence the shaping of policy and the composition of the student body. Scholarship policy might even be connected to program development. For example, new programs might receive a number of scholarships in order to recruit students quickly. Faculty involvement on scholarship selection committees provides the committee with an essential perspective while increasing the faculty member's knowledge of the process. Instructional units might also be granted recruitment and retention scholarship funds. Having access to these resources encourages the department to recruit students that enhance the quality of the program. Retention scholarships act as a tool for retaining students who may be considering stopping out due to circumstances beyond the control of the community college. Supporting instructional units with recruitment and retention by granting them access to scholarship funds encourages instructional units' desire to collaborate in SEM initiatives.

Prerequisites

The establishment and ongoing assessment of the value of prerequisites may be something of a de facto involvement of faculty in SEM when viewed from an academic orientation. Prerequisites clearly shape student progress and success. To serve as an effective element of a SEM plan, a well-developed system for determining a prerequisite and for reviewing continued effectiveness must exist. Student performance is the goal and thus should be used as the key indicator of effectiveness. This learning is often best facilitated by a sound academic advising program that involves program faculty. Faculty plays the central role in determining how well prerequisites support SEM goals.

Prerequisites typically impact enrollment in both the preparation course and the receiving course. Planning for and assessing this enrollment impact is vital for reviewing faculty and classroom requirements. There must be ample opportunity for students to complete prerequisites in order to keep enrollments in receiving courses at an optimal level.

Early Alert Systems

Related to advising, but more targeted in purpose, the rise of early alert systems has engaged faculty in a plan to prevent student withdrawal, improve student performance, and increase course completion. These systems, though they vary in design, require faculty training in recognizing those student behaviors prone to lead to withdrawal or course failure. Typically, these systems arise from reviews of the research on student withdrawal, but also rely on collecting observations from campus faculty concerning their own predictors. Generally, most faculty members are very concerned about students succeeding in their courses. As faculty's awareness of the life issues students are attempting to balance increases, and as they know they are not alone in supporting students, faculty become more likely to participate in making an early alert system a viable SEM tool.

Course Scheduling

Course scheduling is the underlying element in a number of creative efforts by faculty to improve student learning and success. Efforts such as learning communities, intentionally designed cohort models that facilitate access, developmental skill training, or transition programs such as first term/year student and summer bridge programs, receive impetus from an academic orientation to SEM. These kinds of efforts differ from other SEM orientations where scheduling is used to maximize resources or student convenience. Though not appropriate for all academic programs, the design, implementation, and assessment of learning communities and other cohort models is often inspiring for faculty. These programs support improvements in teaching and student performance for targeted student populations. The collaboration with other faculty and clear impact on learning and success exemplifies the teaching mission of most community college faculty.

Co-curricular Programs

Encouraging faculty to serve as advisors and on advisory panels for student organizations is a natural means for promoting student-faculty engagement that supports retention. Facilitating the creation of student groups that complement the classroom experience brings faculty into the lives of students and the campus community, generating a more active learning environment. This is a challenging aspect of a SEM plan that focuses on the involvement of faculty in broad efforts to create a desired community college learning environment. The additional time commitment required by faculty, often with little recognition or compensation represents the most critical challenge to faculty—student engagement through co-curricular activity. However, when motivated students engage in learning outside the classroom, the personal satisfaction of seeing classroom learning applied can be very satisfying.

All the activities listed above support an academic orientation to SEM by focusing on the involvement of instructional leaders, faculty, and academic programs in guiding enrollment and student success goals. Each provides a different opportunity for instruction to embrace SEM in the pursuit of goals mutually shared with the institution and for faculty to contribute more actively to the health of the community college.

CONCLUSION

Numerous experts in the field of SEM have advocated in recent years for a stronger connection to and involvement of the instructional units. This is a difficult challenge given the deep-seated concept of SEM as a structural, goal setting, and service delivery focused effort. However, in the community college, where quality teaching and learning constitutes a crucial aspect for faculty and instructional leaders, enrollment managers may appeal to this value and cultural belief to connect SEM to instructional efforts. The development of a strategic SEM effort concentrates on how the instructional unit of the community college can achieve strong integration of instruction and services, while also creating a learning environment that fully supports student success. Congruence between the strategic goals of the community college, the academic master plan, and the SEM plan generates broad institutional engagement and alignment. Tying SEM to the academic master plan can lead to such congruence and the advancement of SEM concepts by instructional units. Institutional and standardized assessments foster the development of classrooms that support student success and retention, while making data driven pedagogical change.

It must be recognized that the focus of this chapter has been on SEM in relationship with credit course faculty and degree-seeking students. The concepts presented here would benefit from additional input from faculty teaching adult basic skills, workforce training, and small business development; continuing education faculty; and faculty from other educational programs at the community college. Further work is needed to infuse SEM throughout the educational profile of the community college.

SEM will support and enhance the instructional core of the community college mission if we find and engage in relationships at the natural points of common interest. The opportunities to build SEM efforts that connect to faculty described in this chapter are not exhaustive, nor prescriptive, due to the wide range of institutional systems, cultures, and structures. Though SEM in community colleges may not "shape a class" as it might at selective institutions, SEM can shape the potential of our diverse student populations to succeed in any of our academic programs.

4

Data and Decision Making

by Christine Kerlin *and* William Serrata

4

Driven by Frank Kotsonis's exhortation that "the plural of anecdote is not data" the successful enrollment management team will focus heavily on developing and analyzing factual data to drive its decisions. But it is wise to also assert that the plural of "datum" is not "proof." (Ameriwire 2004) Over-reliance on data, without judgment and without reasonable verification and triangulation, can build a shaky foundation for an institutional plan.

These pithy reminders underscore the complexity of gathering and using data for decision making. This chapter will outline important aspects of using data in strategic enrollment management, with some tips for success.

THE CASE FOR USING DATA

Enrollment management requires assessment and decision making. The stakes can be high for many institutions. In some cases, strategies can involve an expensive marketing campaign aimed at claiming a larger presence in a competitive marketplace. Or they may involve the termination of an instructional program in order to expand another program. Strategies could include a realignment of financial aid and scholarship programs to reach more students or the reorganization of student services. Strategies such as these should not be taken without a serious review of the baseline information, the alternatives, and the possible outcomes of such activities; such a review should include strong data. Few of us would enter into these conversations without turning to some sort of data to support arguments for and against various proposals.

The exploration of data also generates ideas and proposals. Often, a trend or an outcome may not be apparent to us until we study data. We may have had to dig for the data, or it may be right in front of us and simply need interpretation. In any case, building a habit of reviewing data can assist enrollment managers and other leaders to think proactively about our challenges and opportunities.

The case for using data also includes the assurance of some level of accountability and transparency. Decisions in areas related to budget, staffing, and institutional direction are certainly open to question, and the support of data, as well as other rationale, are critical to the validity of the process. As data are examined, reviewed, and discussed over time, colleges typically experience increasing levels of responsibility and accountability. This is particularly true at the president's cabinet level.

The importance of data to effective SEM practice has been well documented. Dolence (1998) includes "Improve Access to Information," as a goal of SEM. Bontrager also speaks to the integral role that data plays in SEM. stating "Enrollment management is a complex of concepts and processes that enables the fulfillment of institutional mission and students' educational goals by: creating a data-rich environment to inform decisions and evaluate strategies" (2004a, p. 12).

DATA COLLECTION

Who collects data about a college? Where is the data? In community colleges, data probably hides in many corners. This presents the first challenge: identifying where data is held. It is not unusual to find special programs, such as adult basic education and literacy programs, collecting and storing data regarding entering skill levels and progression through basic classes. The health sciences program, which may use a selective admission method and may need to validate the acquisition of skills, license scores, and graduate placement, may also store data. Naturally, the enrollment services office collects student and enrollment data, as do the financial aid and placement testing offices. The TRIO program office may be collecting data to meet federal grant requirements. The instruction office holds data related to scheduling, faculty load, and program costs. Administrative service offices track tuition and other income. And, of course, the institutional research office, if your campus is lucky enough to have one, gathers and generates all sorts of data and may be the locus for data that supports the IPEDS reports. Finally, a state board or coordinating agency may hold data as well.

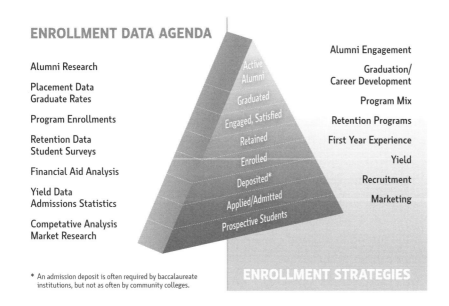

ENROLLMENT DATA AGENDA

Alumni Research

Placement Data
Graduate Rates

Program Enrollments

Retention Data
Student Surveys

Financial Aid Analysis

Yield Data
Admissions Statistics

Competative Analysis
Market Research

Active Alumni
Graduated
Engaged, Satisfied
Retained
Enrolled
Deposited*
Applied/Admitted
Prospective Students

Alumni Engagement

Graduation/
Career Development

Program Mix

Retention Programs

First Year Experience

Yield

Recruitment

Marketing

ENROLLMENT STRATEGIES

* An admission deposit is often required by baccalaureate
institutions, but not as often by community colleges.

◀ FIGURE 4.1

Creating a Data-Driven
Enrollment Plan

SOURCE: BOB
BONTRAGER, 2007

Whether an institution has an institutional research office, or the number of persons employed in such an office if it exists, varies among community colleges. Where institutional research resources are lacking, the college's enrollment manager usually serves as a data collector, distributor, and analyzer. This speaks again to the importance of data in the practice of SEM.

The type of data utilized in SEM is wide-ranging. With respect to the dictum that Strategic Enrollment Management is a "comprehensive process," a college may find itself identifying enrollment issues that range from initial marketing, to applications for admission, to retention, to graduation rates, to alumni outcomes. Figure 4.1 provides a look at the continuum of issues or strategies that should be informed by data and information.

There is no single roadmap for data collection, but it is clear that the first tasks are to identify data locations, the persons responsible, and how to pull it all together. The culture and structure of each campus will call for different collection strategies. Possible options include collaboration with vice presidents to use their knowledge and network to flush out data. If a recent self-study for accreditation purposes has been completed, there will be significant data contained in that text, as well as clues to other sources of data. Collaboration with those who generate IPEDS data will yield a goldmine. In addition, many community colleges make reports and/or submit data to state coordinating offices where not only the college's data can be found, but comparative data as well. Whether the college has a well-staffed office to conduct institutional research or has made institutional research a responsibility of one or more individuals who have multiple responsibilities, it may be wise to identify a point-person to carry the responsibility for assembling the data relevant to enrollment management planning.

Collection of college data is only one aspect, however. External data is equally as important. Local and regional demographics, statewide enrollment trends, financial aid and tuition trends, and a review of competitors, to name a few items, should also be the subject of analysis.

One of the first steps in developing a SEM effort is finding the data and sifting through it. Initial efforts will probably only scrape the surface, but starting the process is critical. As SEM planning matures, so will the process of finding and analyzing more and better data.

DATA ACCURACY AND RELEVANCE

Once over the hurdle of locating data and pulling it together for a review, two other questions emerge: Is the data worth anything? Is the data useful? These questions are answered only after significant cross-checking and analysis.

Since data tends to be collected in many different ways, for many different purposes, it would not be unusual to find that the definitions used to code or to organize data elements are different from sample to sample and office to office within the same college, contributing to a phenomenon known as "dirty data." Perhaps the most difficult hurdle to overcome in the process of using data for planning is identifying how the whole institution can find ways to use common definitions and a common vocabulary. Concurrent with that effort is finding a forum that enables those who generate data and use data to gain sufficient understanding about how others on the same campus do it too. Regular meetings of staff involved in data collection and analysis concerning questions and challenges will help to strengthen the institution's information flow.

Part of the process of determining the usefulness of the data is formulating selected questions and checking to see how different types of data sources respond to such questions. For example, when asking "how many students who enroll part-time are enrolled in morning classes," it is valuable to see if your department data, your institutional research data, and your registrar's data yield the same answer. This "cross-checking" will aid in determining where flaws may lie.

It is not possible to assert that an institution can arrive at a single perfectly controlled system of data collection and analysis, but it is possible to narrow the gaps and create a climate of communication that fosters a broader understanding of the importance of clean, valid, and congruent data.

COLLECTING DATA

The following strategies for collecting, analyzing, and presenting data provide illustrations of how data might be useful in SEM.

Environmental Scan

As an institution engages in enrollment management planning it is valuable to assure that everyone is on the same page in understanding the external challenges and opportunities the institution faces. An environmental scan can support that goal.

Scans vary from institution to institution, but specific topics form the core of a scan: regional demographic trends; local high school enrollments and outcomes; regional competitor institutions; state and national policy trends; state and regional economic trends; occupational outlooks; and tuition and financial aid trends. The institutional research office and/or a team that represents diverse sectors of the college should brainstorm the external factors possibly affecting the college and assemble the data for review.

Sharing the environmental scan and making it the subject of discussion at meetings will build common understandings, perceptions, and an accurate formulation of the issues facing the college. Typically, a scan is renewed every year or two and includes revised information that reflects new directions or new questions.

Factbook

While the environmental scan tends to look outward, a factbook will look inward. A factbook comprises a compilation of enrollment data and other campus trends (perhaps revenue and expenditure trends, financial aid awards, student demographics, etc.) designed to help campus decision makers understand the basics of their enrollment dynamics. An added benefit of a factbook is that it compiles data for consistent use around the college, providing, for example, a common answer to the FTE for fall term, or the part-time/full-time student ratio.

Like the environmental scan, the factbook should be compiled annually—if not more often—and as the years go by will reflect improvements in the kinds of data collected.

A comprehensive factbook, which slices and dices data several different ways, often reveals flaws in the data. Like the scan, it should be reviewed and discussed widely. Doing so usually brings different perspectives that question the methods employed to collect or interpret the data.

Dashboard

Both the scan and the factbook tend to be compendia of data, often prefaced by a summary analysis. A dashboard, on the other hand, may be a series of tables or graphs highlighting key data on a special topic on a single printed page or Web page, which is updated on a regular and frequent basis. The dashboard is intended to provide a quick view of data, much as a glance at the instrumentation on your automobile's dashboard gives you a quick status report; analysis may be located on a subsequent page.

Key Performance Indicators

Often a strategic plan identifies those measures or metrics that indicate if the organization is healthy and/or meeting goals. Key Performance Indicators (KPIs) are not the long list of measurements that may reflect every strategy in a plan. Instead, they are the penultimate metrics that encapsulate the general status of an institution. KPIs might be selected enrollment figures, balances on an income and revenue report, completed student applications for a selective program, or the amount of scholarship dollars available. KPIs will reflect the priorities of the specific institution or organization.

KPIs should be tracked and reported regularly. Like the dashboard, they enable leaders to take the temperature of the organization quickly, and identify any requirements for further action or investigation.

Benchmarking

An enrollment management plan should be aligned with the college's strategic plan and with its mission. In that respect, each college's goals will be unique, designed relative to its own context. On the other hand, it is not unusual to ask "What are other colleges doing?' when wondering what goals should be set. Retention rates serve as a good example. Given the current pressure on institutions to retain students and publish high completion rates, schools are examining their own retention rates and wondering if they are exceeding the norm or lagging behind.

"Benchmarking is the process of measuring an organization's internal processes then identifying, understanding, and adapting outstanding practices from other organizations considered to be best-in-class" (Benchnet 2009). As enrollment management teams identify the issues facing their college, it may be helpful to search for benchmarks among peer institutions to determine where their own college's performance is relative to others. Likely areas of interest in benchmarking might be retention rates, graduation rates, tuition rates, waiver or discount programs, support services, and staffing.

While benchmarking is informative, it can be perilous. Data from other institutions may have been defined and collected differently than another's, and comparisons can be shaky. National data, which may purport a basis on equivalent definitions, may belie certain contextual issues that make it less comparable to one's own institution. Consulting directly with peer institutions to gain insight into their experience, attending conferences, and reviewing the literature will help to broaden one's understanding about best practices that may be applicable to the current situation and goals.

Special Reports

The foregoing types of data collection form the backbone of data needed by an institution in its SEM planning, implementation, and assessment. Nonetheless, an institution requires a wide variety of reports to assist in more focused decision-making and tracking. Because SEM is a comprehensive, institution-wide process, the type and quality of reports will vary widely. Each office or department needs to ensure the effective collection and organization of data.

Typical reports include daily, weekly, or quarterly tracking of applications and registrations; placement test results; financial aid applications and awards; waitlists, retention and/or degrees awarded; and surveys, studies, and focus group results, just to name a few. These are valuable to those accountable for key activities and goals of the SEM efforts.

DATA TOOLS

The marketplace is awash with software and systems that support efforts to enter, collate, and present data. Each institution must choose its own tools and mesh its business rules (policies, procedures, and practices) with the parameters of the software. For those institutions that have a longstanding system, the work of assuring that the data that goes in and comes out has probably assumed some level of predictability, thus aiding efforts in managing this data. Those institutions making a change to a new system often find themselves changing data definitions, and may have to look in diverse places for data they once collected a different way.

It is not unusual for an institution to recognize that it cannot manage its planning activities and efficiently conduct its operations with an aging data system, and to embark on the purchase and implementation of a new system. While this is necessary, some delays in actively tracking an enrollment management plan while realigning daily practices related to data reporting may result. It cannot be said strongly enough that a SEM plan—to say nothing of the other planning processes of a college—needs to be based on reliable and accurate data.

Software is also available to attract data. For example, customer relations management (CRM) software creates portal opportunities for prospective students, and others, to provide a wealth of data that can be used to inform an institution of possible new directions in marketing. Using social networks will also drive people to the college and provide analytics as well, thus building another source of data.

Software and its related information systems, of course, are the purveyors of the types of data needed for enrollment management. For this reason, including colleagues knowledgeable about the data systems is critical to the enrollment management effort. This includes not only those who understand the system, but those who manage data entry and reports.

Those institutions that are attempting to sort out their options in developing or purchasing data management systems or software may find that attendance at professional meetings, such as AACRAO's SEM and technology conferences, will provide a showcase of those options, as well as sessions where colleagues from other institutions describe their experiences with new adoptions. AACRAO's professional journal, *College and University*, frequently features articles that provide insight into tools for data collection and management.

DATA ANALYSIS

Up to this point, emphasis has been placed on the collection and presentation of data. Experienced educational leaders know, though, that pages of data—even data that has been carefully collected—do not tell the whole story.

The mantra of "data-driven decisions" should be interpreted to include not only reliance on hard numbers, but on the value given those numbers, the context, and the meaning. This chapter opened with a reference to triangulation, a term used in social science research. Triangulation is a "method of cross-checking data from multiple sources to search for regularities in the research data" (O'Donoghue and Punch 2003, p. 78). By using more than one approach to assessing the data, stronger confidence in the determination of what the data means may occur. As a practical matter, this enables decision makers to weigh the data they are seeing with their experience and with other related information. For example, in the state of Washington the initial implementation of an online application for admission for the community colleges allowed the applicant to simultaneously apply to several schools at once, resulting in a ballooning of applications, many of which were more whimsical than serious. Anyone looking at the weekly application figures would assume a suddenly large incoming enrollment unless the additional information on the source of the increase was reviewed.

As indicated in Figure 4.2, SEM efforts require collaboration among many across campus to provide experience and insight so that data truly becomes information. As a SEM team becomes more practiced in its collection and analysis of data, a richer history of information will develop. This can lead to the ability to build predictive

FIGURE 4.2 ▶

Collecting Information
Through Collaboration

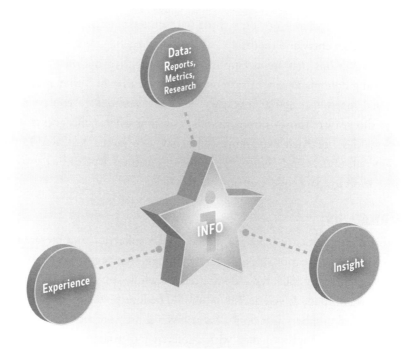

models to support decision making. Computerized systems that incorporate trend data can assist enrollment managers in making projections and doing what-if scenarios, as well as monitoring KPIs.

When does information become noise? When does analysis become paralysis? These are relevant questions in enrollment management. As leaders of an enrollment management effort spend the necessary time to assure that they are reviewing solid data, and as they transform that data into information, it is easy to get lost in a continuous round of asking more questions, seeking more data, conducting more studies or surveys, and then discussing the findings. It is possible to unduly defer decisions in favor of another round of data analysis.

There is no easy answer to these questions. The challenge is to find the point at which decisions are reasonable and results can be measured. As noted in the chapter on Leadership, the enrollment management process is cyclical and requires an assessment process. As many enrollment managers can attest, even those decisions made on strong data after considerable deliberation do not always have the predicted outcome. Enrollment management planning is filled with continuous review and revision as more information comes into play.

DATA DANGERS

While data and their analysis serve as a pillar for strategic enrollment management, it must also be noted that data can serve as an impediment to effective SEM practice. Data dangers include the data cycle, analysis paralysis, and data detachment. Enrollment managers must be aware of data dangers on their respective campuses.

The Data Cycle

Data and more appropriately the analysis of relevant data play a pivotal role in Strategic Enrollment Management at all levels of higher education, and the community college sector is no exception. However as an institution becomes a connoisseur of the data, it must also expect delays along the way specifically dealing with the data.

Many institutions will be forced to deal with the "data cycle," surprisingly similar to the five stages of grief.[1]

- **DENIAL**—Upon thorough review of SEM benchmarks for participation, retention, or success, if the data is less than flattering, the dean or administrator responsible for the data will often deny accuracy of the data. Many times the statement will be, "this data can't be right," or "that may be the institutional data but it is not accurate for my division or department."

- **ANGER**—As discussion of the data progresses and the accuracy of the information is proven, anger follows as the next stage in the data cycle. The responsible person becomes visibly upset at the data and often at the messenger. Additionally, the anger usually flows over to the students themselves—"it's the students fault," or "if we only had better students my numbers would look better."

- **BARGAINING**—This stage of the data cycle includes praying that the data gets better all by itself, buying time in the hope that the next set of numbers will look more favorable.

---

[1] See www.essortment.com/all/stagesofgri_rvkg.htm

- **DEPRESSION**—As awareness of the reality of the data spreads and becomes visible to more and more of the college staff, the dean or administrator responsible will experience a kind of depression about the data. Frustration with students, enrollment staff and processes, and self-pity based on a feeling of hopelessness are all present during this state of the data cycle. The person responsible does not see how the data can improve, as they lack control over the students coming into their respective programs. This is especially true at "open-admission" community colleges.
- **ACCEPTANCE**—Finally the dean or administrator responsible, as well as the rest of the college staff, come to accept the data and begin to focus on strategies that collectively can improve the outcomes being measured. However, it must be noted that the data cycle may take long periods of time to overcome.

Analysis Paralysis

Another danger of data within the context of SEM is analysis paralysis. The data presented to decision makers must tell a story and have a clear meaning. All too often, the data and the presentation of the data lead to more questions than answers. A sample of such questions follows:

- Is the data the same for full-time versus part-time students?
- Day students versus night students?
- College-ready versus remedial students?
- Fall versus spring students?
- This year versus last year?
- This major versus that major?
- Academic students versus technical students?
- This campus versus that campus? (For multi-campus community colleges)
- This community college compared to others?

Enrollment managers should have a strong grasp of the data presented and be ready for follow-up questions. A lack of preparation or understanding of the data will lead to additional questions and doubt, therefore leading to a delay in decision making.

Data Detachment

Enrollment managers must always remember that the data presented is so much more than numbers. It is, all too often, easy to get lost amongst the data and forget what—and more specifically whom—the data represent. The data represents a person—a person that may be the first in their family to attempt higher education, a recent immigrant, a single mother, or a laid-off factory worker seeking a new career.

Enrollment managers must remain steadfast that the data represents the students we are privileged to serve; ultimately, the data must be utilized to facilitate student success.

SUMMARY

Data drives good decisions, and is especially critical when decisions may impact financial and human resources, programs, and services. Enrollment managers should work toward assuring the validity and reliability of data, and involve colleagues across campus in collecting and reviewing internal and external data. Facts and figures alone, though, are not sufficient for good decision making. Transforming data into information, and reasonably analyzing it, constitute core challenges for the enrollment manager.

5

BUILDING EFFECTIVE COMMUNITY COLLEGE/
University Partnerships

by Bruce Clemetsen

5 Partnerships serve as a vital element of the strategic enrollment management effort of any community college. Partnerships shape enrollments through access to specific markets, building bridges with community businesses and organizations, strengthening the potential success of a student, and producing efficiencies. Community colleges are the natural link to serve students as they move from one organization to another, through the community college, in pursuit of a goal.

Partnerships require collaboration, but they involve more than a mere collaborative effort. According to Wikipedia, "A partnership is a type of business entity in which partners (owners) share with each other the profits or losses of the business undertaking in which all have invested" (2009). Partnership is the legal definition of the type of relationship described above. It commonly involves a contract delineating the terms of the enterprise, resource contributions expected from each partner, and the terms of continuation and sharing of the success and failure of the effort. The National Coalition for Homeless Veterans (2009) clearly differentiates between a partnership and collaboration:

A legal partnership is a contractual relationship involving close cooperation between two or more parties having specified and joint rights and responsibilities. Each party has an equal share of the risk as well as the reward.

A collaboration involves cooperation in which parties are not necessarily bound contractually. There is a relationship, but it is usually less formal than a binding, legal contract and responsibilities may not be shared equally. A collaboration exists when several people pool their common interests, assets, and professional skills to promote broader interests for the community's benefit. The most important thing to remember is: organizations do not collaborate—*people* collaborate.

THE IMPORTANCE OF PARTNERSHIPS TO COMMUNITY COLLEGES

A search for "community college partnerships" using Google finds 29,600,000 links to related websites (2009). With such prolific use of the term, a SEM professional may wonder if partnerships are a fad, a relabeling of collaborations, or if there is really a commitment to organizational relationships that involve the facilitation of the enterprise with shared gain and loss. We believe that partnerships are a core element of any community college's strategic plan. Partnerships are vital for enrollment growth and stability.

Robert Glenn notes several current forces that are reshaping existing relationships and bringing together organizations that have never worked together in ways to meet emerging mutual goals and social expectations. These include cost containment and elimination of duplicative services; alignment of the full educational enterprise and lifelong learning with an emphasis on improving student learning and progress; needing to define the institution in an increasingly competitive environment; leveraging of internet resources; and expectations for the development between educational institutions of new, functional, student-centered efforts to meet demands for improved educational attainment that support economic development (Glenn 2008, p. 2). It may be argued that community colleges have the concept of partnership built into their cultures as they were formed out of the community as a partner to create access for local citizens based on the local culture and goals. Still today, the vitality of the community college movement is grounded in its ability to partner. The evidence is plentiful, and future success, like success of the past, will be determined by the ability to develop partnerships that tie the community college to the community, economic development, access opportunities for students in high school, developing access and success pathways to employment for the full range of diverse people in our community, and facilitating successful transfer to the university.

Before engaging in a partnership, each organization must ask itself some critical questions about the commitment. A community college would benefit from the conversations directed towards answering the following:

- What is the goal of the partnership, and does that goal support the mission of the institution?
- What does the partnership add or improve related to compelling strategic goals of the institution, specifically in this case, enrollment and student success goals?
- What is the central focus of the partnership, and what are the values that will guide decisions about organizational changes required to produce the desired success?
- How will the partnership create a competitive advantage for each partner?
- What level of institutional leadership supports the partnership?
- What is the vision of how the partnership may evolve?
- How will the partnership foster new opportunities as it evolves?
- What organizational leadership is committed to building ongoing relationships with colleagues with the partner organization? Are the right people in the room?

The author acknowledges that the singular focus on partnering with universities is an incomplete view of the partnership role of a community college. The relative position of the community college as supporter of high school completion, workforce development and retraining, and other education functions places community colleges in a position to be good organizational citizens by being true partners with a diverse array of organizations. Community colleges provide the base that supports educational attainment and economic development. SEM professionals build partnering capacity and capitalize on their college's relationships to create pathways and generate enrollments that support learner, partner organization, and community goals. The successful partnerships community colleges have built with high schools, workforce agencies, businesses, and others are worthy of chapters of their own. The remainder of this chapter will focus on the relationship with universities as a strategic partnership for improving the transfer function of community colleges.

PARTNERSHIPS AND SEM

It seems clear that partnerships hold a number of generalized benefits. However, what value does partnering play in the SEM professional's efforts to meet the enrollment goals of the community college? Glenn (2008) provides a cogent guide for developing a SEM strategy based on efforts to design shared enrollment services. Understanding that a partnership involves a sharing of service delivery, Glenn's paper offers relevant factors to assess when forming partnerships. Given the critical need for data sharing and communication and coordination, it is critical to determine the compatibility of institutions' information systems to support a partnership. Policies and procedures must be evaluated and revised to support the desired outcome of a partnership. Those leading an effort to form a partnership are advised to develop a student-centered approach suppressing a "we're different" attitude that limits options. Efforts must be made to understand service expectations and abilities among partners, acknowledging that discrepancies will be discovered and trusting that feedback about performance differences is intended to foster improvement. Finally, partners must examine internal perspectives and concern about a perceived loss of a competitive advantage as a result of any partnership. The individuals involved in creating the partnership must be able to confront the idea, often inaccurate, that student enrollments are being sacrificed. Partners must articulate how the partnership, and each institution's investment, results in a new, meaningful competitive advantage.

The ways that partnerships benefit SEM also can be viewed from the four orientations to enrollment management offered by David Kalsbeek (2006a). From a marketing perspective, partnerships can be utilized to access and maintain a prominent position in a particular niche. Administratively, partnerships can result in efficiencies and enhanced effectiveness in serving various student populations. In addition, enhanced academic program development can arise from partnerships with organizations that are developing new markets and industries that will require new types of skills in the labor force. It is important to recognize the potential for partnerships to influence student access and success through the connection to a support system among institutions and/or agencies that together provide more and different support than when encountered separately. A community college's ability to be a good partner and develop diverse partnerships constitutes a strategic advantage that enrollment managers ought to make a centerpiece of any SEM plan.

Partnerships can be a strategic advantage for academic program development—developing markets to increase access and building programs that enhance student success. Community colleges connect to high schools through various programs that support high achieving students and open doors to those who did not believe they would be academically or socially able to go to college. Partnerships with business and industry have resulted in strong training programs to keep businesses competitive and community members employed, as well as ensuring that community colleges remain on the cutting edge of developing academic programs for emergent business needs and new industries. Many community colleges have strong partnerships with community agencies that collectively support the Workforce Investment Act, building pathways for retraining and living wage employment. The relationship with universities is yet another potentially powerful partnership to facilitate the ever-growing demand for a workforce of individuals with at least a bachelor's degree. While not an exhaustive list, it does reflect the diverse opportunities for enrollment managers to maximize the success of students and support the mission of the community college.

THE COMMUNITY COLLEGE–UNIVERSITY PARTNERSHIP

The relationship between community colleges and universities is well established. The transfer function of the community college is widespread and frequently valued as a core element of the mission of many community colleges. Reports like "The Road Less Traveled? Students Who Enroll in Multiple Institutions" (Peter and Cataldi 2005) reflect the growing movement of students among institutions, resulting in challenges to traditional accountability measures for a 2+2 model of student transfer. Community colleges, universities, and state systems respond in various ways to improve the transfer relationship in order to improve transfer student performance, associate and baccalaureate degree attainment, persistence, reduce credit loss, reduce time to degree, and reduce student frustration with repeating classes and seemingly burdensome bureaucracy. For these reasons, SEM leaders in community colleges must play a vital role in initiating, shaping, and evolving the efforts to support the transfer mission of the institution.

The current financial and political environments are catalysts for furthering SEM plans that look to increasing the transfer student population through strong relationships with universities. Financially, transfer students typically represent some of the lowest cost and, therefore, greatest net revenue enrollments. In the political

FIGURE 5.1 ▶

The Two-Year/
Four-Year
Relationship
Continuum

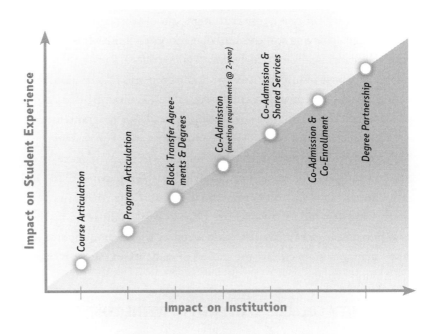

realm, great interest in increasing baccalaureate degree attainment arises from the desire to maintain a global economic advantage. Additionally, several other political issues contribute to growing transfer support arrangements including, credit transferability, time-to-degree, degree (associate and bachelor's) completion, and access to bachelor's degrees for low-income and underrepresented groups. Enrollment managers at community colleges whose missions include a transfer component would be wise to assess continuously their relationships with universities.

The responses to this call from diverse, and at times competing, stakeholders for improvement in this area have resulted in a continuum of relationships among two- and four-year institutions (See Figure 5.1).

Each of these relationships supports students and the transfer mission of the community college. The nature of the work, breadth and level of personnel involved, and complexity increase with each component of the continuum. The impact and success of any of these types of relationships depends on the connection to the community college's SEM strategy regarding transfer students.

The institutional relationships listed above differ in the breadth of programs and personnel involved; therefore, each has a different impact on students and institutions. It is important to be intentional in pursuing institutional relationships, knowing your starting point on this continuum, connecting to those with the proper authority to enhance the relationship, and having a long-term view of how the relationship may benefit both institutions. Each type of partnership is described below.

Articulation agreements between two- and four-year institutions have been the basis of the longstanding transfer relationship, the basis upon which all other relationships are supported in the two-year/four-year continuum. This necessitates an academic pathway that brings institutions together. The creation of course articulation agreements typically involves select faculty and the services involved in reviewing and implementing articulation. These agreements aid in setting a foundation for a student pathway that links institutions, but these agreements may change regularly with little or no requirement that both institutions invest making any operational change to support the agreement. Though the agreement assists students, the focus of the relationship entails the assessment and acknowledgement of curricular congruence.

Establishing program articulations requires a stronger relationship between faculty at the two institutions to develop a more enduring, comprehensive, and potentially unique arrangement for students. Program articulations may be motivated by a number of reasons. In relation to SEM, they are helpful for pursuing new student markets or providing easier transfers for students already moving between specific institutional programs. With respect to the relationship continuum, students experience better service, the institutions communicate, and a student pathway is established, however, institutions have not transformed themselves in order to support more than credit transfer.

To facilitate credit transfer many states and some institutions have established block transfer degrees. These degrees provide the community college graduate with some benefit upon transfer to the university. Completion of the block transfer degree, often an associate of arts degree, may result in guaranteed admission or junior standing for registration purposes, assurance that all lower division general education requirements are satisfied. These degrees increase the articulation relationship as both institutions must continually negotiate new courses that best serve students through the degree program. Community college enrollment managers must engage with their counterparts at the university to ensure that course development at both institutions optimally supports students not losing credits and that students are well prepared for upper division coursework. These types of degree programs can foster more intense and frequent contacts between institutional personnel as a result of external pressures to work effectively together to reduce credit loss and time to degree.

The growth of co-admission programs reflects advancing relationships between two- and four-year institutions. These programs vary in whether a student is admitted after some success at the two-year institution or at the initial time of entering the community college and required to meet and maintain certain performance standards in order to matriculate eventually at the university. Co-admission programs impact enrollment managers as they begin to affect institutional roles and systems. The community college will have to wrestle with recruitment questions if it sees the co-admission agreement as offering a new program that can open new markets or increase access to existing markets. Good communication and referral must be established between admission offices. Admission and advising staff may need to learn more about the policies and procedures of each institution. In addition, attention paid to articulation becomes more intense in order to facilitate student success when matriculating. Community college resources dedicated to student success become vital in assuring that sufficient students enter the university through the program. Co-admission programs are the first phase of the relationship continuum that causes a shift in institutional practices, reflecting a developing partnership.

A model where students are co-admitted and allowed access to some services at the university represents another step towards a two-year and four-year partnership. Typically, students may be allowed access to residence halls, recreation centers, libraries, or other services that support the creation of a more well rounded experience than a student might find at the community college. This relationship introduces students to the collegiate lifestyle many traditional age students seek, bringing more opportunity for marketing options by the community college. These types of amenities are shared resources that allow the community college to better attract a demographic looking for the benefits of the community college learning environment and affordability, but who also desire a fuller student experience outside the classroom.

When co-enrollment is combined with co-admission, enrollment managers can face new challenges and realize new opportunities. The most prominent challenge often emerges from the perceived need to restrict when a student can begin taking classes at the university so as to not lose enrollment-based funding and tuition. Their university counterparts will also have to confront perceptions that students are being taken away by the community college. As described at the beginning of this chapter, if both institutions make the investment in the relationship and understand the benefits over acting more independently, these concerns can be adequately addressed. The opportunity present in this type of program is the ability of students, and stakeholders, to see that the partner university holds the quality of education at the community college in high esteem. This creates new marketing potential and enrollment growth opportunity. The support of co-enrollment has implications for student success efforts as well. Peter and Carroll (2005) found in a National Center for Educational Statistics study that "Students who began in public 2-year institutions who had co-enrolled had higher rates of bachelor's degree attainment and persistence at 4-year institutions than their counterparts who did not co-enroll" (p. 19). Co-enrollment at a two-year and a four-year institution for at least one month resulted in persistence and graduation rates similar to those of students who attended a single four-year institution. This arrangement expands the diversity of student services and academic affairs units that need to work together to develop systems and guidelines for supporting successful student movement between institutions.

The most advanced type of relationship between two- and four-year institutions is the degree partnership. This involves co-admission, unrestricted co-enrollment, coordinated financial aid, open access to student services, highly coordinated articulation and block transfer agreements, and unique academic program offerings as a result of the support for the student's whole experience and academic collegiality between faculties. The purpose of this type of program is to expand educational opportunity and bachelor degree completion (Bontrager, Clemetsen, and Watts 2005).

Degree partnerships are in essence their own SEM programs, influencing virtually all aspects of the community college as students begin to see the two institutions as one. Students view the programs and services of both institutions as a combined set of offerings, over which each student experiences increased control in shaping their educational program and experiences (Clemetsen and Balzer 2008). Balzer (2006) found that students understood the value of the university identity, but appreciated the smaller scale of the educational environment, focus on teaching, and strong support services of the community college. A model for this level of partnership is exhibited in an eleven-year program between Linn-Benton Community College and Oregon State University. This program has seen an annual increase in applications and enrollments every year with positive enrollment outcomes at both institutions, including increases in student numbers, persistence, and degree completion. In spite of these successes, or perhaps because of them, students, faculty, and staff at both institutions continue to press for and create ever-expanding educational opportunities. This type of partnership has great influence on SEM as it produces new academic offerings, opens new marketing and recruiting opportunities, facilitates student educational goals, and becomes an institutional trademark.

The relationship with the university sector is a vital element in any SEM effort for those community colleges with a transfer component in their missions. The relationship shapes the impact on SEM planning and decisions. Focusing on students' educational experience versus institutional issues can result in growing a partnership that significantly alters systems, programs, and student experiences for increased support of student success.

It should be noted that the development of a partnership with a university is truly only one-half of the equation for strategically enhancing the achievement of students' intent for a bachelor's degree; the other half of the equation is strong partnerships with high schools. Partnerships with high schools include strong dual credit programs, advanced placement (AP) articulation, high school completion with college credit programs, and bridge programs. Partnerships that facilitate high school completion and early college credit accumulation that progresses a student towards postsecondary degree completion offer hope and access to many young people who would never consider pursuing college.

CONCLUSION

A community college may find excelling at partnering a strategy to build upon as an integral component of a SEM initiative. To maximize the potential for partnering, identification and assessment of the relationships with community agencies, educational institutions, businesses, and others provide a community college with a clear sense of where growth and opportunity exist. Key to developing this strategy is finding relationships with a common focus on student success and an equal willingness to invest scarce resources to leverage the talents of both organizations to create something new that is a competitive advantage for each partner or contributes to mutual mission critical achievement.

A partnership between a community college and a university can create a competitive advantage when focused on student success through the integration of academic programs and student services. The paradox of a partnership is how the investment in common educational commitments and values results in the emergence of unique experiences for students and programs supporting community development.

Partnerships that create novel solutions to systemic problems or new models that depart from long-held paradigms are subject to misunderstanding and disbelief. The SEM professional and his colleagues must assist others in changing their vision of the educational enterprise—how success is defined, how service is delivered, and more importantly, how students experience education.

6

Marketing
ommunity Colleges

by Alicia Moore *and* Ron Paradis

6   When a president, dean, or faculty member asks for help in marketing, he or she most likely seeks a miraculous promotional plan to help
shore up enrollment either college wide or for a specific program—
and generally, results are expected immediately. True marketing,
however, is a systematic approach, involving a much more holistic process. Michael
Levens supports this assertion by stating, "marketing is an organizational function
and a collection of processes designed to plan for, create, communicate and deliver
value to customers and to build effective customer relationships in ways that benefit
the organization" (2010, p. 267). Countless other resources emphasize that a true
marketing plan extends far beyond direct promotion of the institution or of a specific academic program. Truly integrated marketing "extends to the strategic matter
of product, place, price/cost, convenience and the customer" (Black 2004, p. 7).
Despite this, community colleges, through enrollment managers and public relations directors, are too often focused solely on promotion—sometimes by choice,
sometimes by internal politics—and ignore these other critical influences.

Similarly, many in higher education look at strategic enrollment management
simply as a recruiting plan, supported by promotional activities. However, if a campus truly embraces the concept of SEM and has developed a thoughtful SEM plan,
then enrollment managers, public relations directors, and their colleagues will be in a
unique position to influence academic program mix, tuition, retention, and the like.
Using this as a basis for discussion, this chapter will demonstrate how a fully supported SEM plan is integral to the development of an integrated marketing plan.

UNDERSTANDING THE MARKETING MIX

Colleges and universities—through enrollment managers or public relations offices—generally excel at developing view books or promotional brochures; instituting communication plans; designing recruiting events; and employing direct marketing techniques such as email, text messaging, or, more recently, social networking. All of these represent good marketing strategies—or to be more precise, all of these are good promotional efforts.

In truth, however, promotion is just one of the four "Ps" that make up an integrated marketing plan, essential to the effective selling of the product. Most basic definitions of marketing begin with the "marketing mix," sometimes referred to as the four "Ps": product, place, price, and promotion. Marketing professionals in the business sector delve daily into this mix and help shape all of the marketing components of the products and companies with whom they work. Moreover, they are acutely aware that a "failure in one marketing mix variable could undermine good choices made with the other marketing mix variable" (Levens 2001, p. 9) and having cross-sector representation when determining each of the "Ps" is critical to success. What most in academia seem reluctant to admit is that those with responsibility for developing the campus marketing plan, unlike their business sector peers, generally have little influence over the first three parts of this model. Rather, institutional organizational structures or internal campus politics regarding "turf" often limit whose voices are heard in recommending product (*i.e.*, academic programs) and place (*i.e.*, satellite campuses, weekend or online courses) to instructional leadership. Similarly, the institution's budget office generally determines price (*i.e.*, tuition) based solely on budget considerations. In contrast to these approaches, placing the four "Ps" into the context of SEM allows for cross-campus influence on all four aspects.

Kalsbeek and Hossler assert that "marketing as a process and a discipline has become inextricably intertwined with the practice of enrollment management and the language of marketing is a natural part of the [enrollment management] lexicon" (2009, p. 4). SEM, when done right, can have significant influence—if not set direction entirely—over all four of the important "P" components of the marketing mix. Moreover, an integrated SEM and marketing plan requires an additional "P": people—the right people—leading and advocating for a process that shapes the

SEM plan and showcases important considerations in determining price, product, place, and promotion.

PRODUCT

The name of the product or entity constitutes the primary component of the first "P" in the business world, which could be the brand or the specific product name within that brand. To illustrate, Proctor and Gamble represents the brand, while Crest, Pampers, and Gillette are the specific products. Similarly, in higher education, the brand may be California Polytechnic State University, San Luis Obispo, while the product may be their engineering program. In addition, while community colleges may struggle for such national recognition, they stand for a significant and widely-recognized brand within their surrounding communities. One only needs to look at the impact of each community college in its service district to recognize the popularity of the community college brand.

Most in higher education struggle to see education as a product. However, it is important to remember that a product is not always something tangible. As noted by Barbara Findly Schenck, "Services are products, too.... The only difference between services and tangible products is that you can see and touch the tangible product before you buy it, whereas with services you commit to the purchase before you see the outcomes of your decision" (2001, p. 267). Services can include legal, financial, and medical services—and of course, education.

The business sector spends considerable time and energy defining its product and understanding its market position. Generally very skilled at doing the same, four-year institutions have a long-standing history in similar exercises, albeit through the use of Carnegie classifications; institutional profiles using SAT/ACT scores, high school GPAs, demographic data, and other factors; IPEDS data; or innumerable other methods. Many of these tools, however, rely on data not traditionally used or available at community colleges and as such, community colleges often struggle with defining their product in relationship to peer institutions. Keeping institutional mission central to all discussions—which not so coincidentally is also the central element of the SEM definition provided throughout this book—will provide community colleges with guidance in better defining its product and its marketplace. Key questions for this discussion include:

- Does the institutional mission align with community needs?
- Does the institutional mission align with the programs and services offered?
- Does the institutional mission align with the needs of the different market segments within the college service district?
- Does the entirety of the institution understand and embrace the institution's mission?

Central to the definition of a successful SEM plan is insuring that the institutional mission corresponds to students' educational needs. If an institution can affirmatively answer the above questions, then the institution has made significant strides towards SEM success—but it cannot stop there. Rather, in order to fully define the product, a SEM team must collectively participate in the collection and analysis of data to allow the development of appropriate SEM strategies. It is only when an institution's SEM team successfully navigates through all aspects of the SEM model that the full product can be defined. To state this more overtly, student services and instructional representatives must work together to understand and analyze data supporting SEM goals as they relate to one another's areas and provide input as to possible strategies to reach those goals. Simply said, both areas must "play well in the sandbox together" in order to develop the best product and associated strategies possible.

Defining the product is the most critical aspect of the first element of the marketing mix. Other considerations include addressing appearance, packaging, functionality, perceived quality, warranty, and support services. Briefly defined in the context of community colleges below, these elements round out discussions regarding the product's definition (that is, the institutional mission) and complement the data analysis and strategy development phase of a SEM process.

- **PRODUCT MIX:** While community colleges do not package themselves similar to Proctor and Gamble, they do offer a wide range of products to consumers. Unlike universities which would list undergraduate education, graduate education, service, and research as primary products, community colleges have a wider range: credit and non-credit classes; transfer and career and technical education programs; degrees and certificates; pre-college offerings including adult basic education, developmental classes, and English language learning; service to the community; and so forth.

APPEARANCE: As with other services, most people do not think of education in terms of packaging. However, appearance is important and is showcased in how the institution portrays itself to its constituents in everything from its logo and advertising images to how well the campus buildings and grounds are maintained.

FUNCTIONALITY: How does the college "work?" Are the admission and registration processes easy to understand and complete? Are the services to students appropriate and useful? Are academic support services appropriate to meet student need, and are they accessible? Do credits transfer as promised?

PERCEIVED QUALITY: While value is important to students (as our customers), so too is quality. Levens states that "consumers will pay for a product (or service) only if it has an adequate level of quality at a fair price" (2010, p. 47). Community colleges struggle to overcome the often-held belief that the colleges provide subpar education. Rather, a fully developed SEM plan, one supported by the full marketing mix, will assist in portraying community colleges as viable options for those wishing to pursue higher education.

WARRANTY: While use of the term "warranty" may seem awkward when talking about higher education, it ultimately refers to the brand or product's promise. David Kalsbeek explores this concept and states, "students enroll with a sense of the institution's brand promise—that their enrollment is a function of their assessment, however accurate or sophisticated, of how that brand promise meshes with their own goals, values and aspiration" (2006b, p. 4). While some community colleges actually offer tangible options for those who do not find a job post-graduation, most community "warranties" simply give a promise of future careers or ability to transfer and pursue a bachelor's degree. Therefore, warranties do not always need to be tangible in nature, but can be implied.

● **SUPPORT SERVICES:** It is not just about the quality of the product but what comes with the purchase. Electronics giant Best Buy offers access to the "Geek Squad" if customers experience problems or technical issues. Similarly, community colleges offer other types of support, including advising, tutoring, mental health counseling, campus activities, financial aid, and other services in support of the education process.

PRICE

Price, on its surface, seems like a fairly simple concept: how much does a student pay for his or her classes? A multitude of differing funding streams, external politics, pressure to remain "affordable" (however that might be defined), competition with nearby peer institutions, and other pressures often make "pricing" difficult in the community college environment. However, a strong institution-wide SEM planning process can tremendously influence the pricing discussion.

At its most fundamental level, Sevier (2003) defines the "price" discussion in terms of gross price (the "sticker" price that students use to compare one college to another), net price (the cost after aid), and reservation price (the real or psychological price point that students or their families will not pay). While it is the goal to get the net price below the reservation price, the pricing discussion must take other factors into account, especially in community colleges where there is little variance in the final tuition and fee structure amongst peer institutions.

In the business sector, price determination also includes consideration of sale price or discounts, financing options, and loss leaders. Many of these apply to the higher education arena, although they often appear using different terminology. Sale prices or discounts can be equated to tuition discounting, a topic which has been well documented and will not receive in-depth exploration here. Brief examples, however, include the use of scholarships or discounts for specific populations (*e.g.*, athletes, students from specific high schools, seniors) and reduced tuition for certain programs.

Financing options align with financial aid packaging and financial aid leveraging. While many community colleges do not have opportunities to engage in significant financial aid leveraging strategies, at the very least, financial aid offices should interact with those campus departments responsible for delivering campus scholarships.

How, when, and to whom scholarships are awarded—no matter how little or how few are available—is vital to the recruitment and retention of students. Additionally, community colleges are urged to consider at what point they package aid, even loans, as compared to their peers. Considerations include not only when students are notified of their aid award (*i.e.*, financial aid software is generally available in March of each year; how long after this is it loaded and processing for next year begins?), but how long it takes the college to turn around a student's application, as well as the quality of communications. With this, community colleges should also build communication plans that specifically address post-award, but pre-acceptance or pre-enrollment, strategies.

A simple definition of loss leaders is the sale of items at a reduced cost in order to generate customers in other areas. Institutions frequently review which courses generate a profit and which courses benefit from that profit in their academic or SEM planning. SEM can not only inform those discussions, but also those in areas such as discounted courses for high school students, summer "bridge" programs, discount for courses offered at certain times of the day or week, and related areas.

While the above considerations are worthwhile in the pricing/tuition decision process, budget realities often ultimately dictate tuition levels. SEM, on the other hand, can help determine whether tuition should be increased systematically, or whether other options such as program-specific fees, nonresident tuition rates, and tuition discounting should be employed. Moreover, using a SEM lens, some institutions have been able to set a SEM goal to quantify the ratio of gift aid to cost of attendance in order to keep overall cost to the student as low as possible.

That being said, many marketing professionals will say that the concept of value outweighs the actual price. And, even more important than value, is perceived value. At the most basic level, customers make a purchase decision based on the product's perceived value. Findly Schenck carries this further to define value as the sum of price, quality, features, convenience, reliability, expertise, and support. "People buy the $4 loaf of salt-crusted rosemary bread because it satisfies their sense of worldliness and self indulgence. They opt for the high-end sedan for the feeling of prestige and luxury it delivers. They pay top price for legal, advertising, or even accounting services because they like having their name on a prestigious client roster, or maybe because they simply like or trust the attorneys, advertisers, or CPAs more than the people who provided the lower cost estimate" (2001, p. 42). So, too, it goes in higher education when individuals opt for private institutions over community colleges or public universities simply due to the perceived value of the more expensive option. Community colleges must continually demonstrate their value to students, some of which will be defined through the discussion on product and reinforced through the other "Ps" of the marketing mix, but clearly all will be defined through a robust SEM process.

PLACE

Place is comprised of both the location of the product or service and how readily it is available. In the case of toothpaste or soft drinks, place can refer to which stores carry the product and where in the store it is displayed. Coke and Pepsi, for example, spend considerable time, effort, and money to secure prime store locations—particularly in the summer months and near holiday weekends. Different companies in the cosmetic industry utilize significantly different strategies for place in their marketing mix. For example, some receive wide distribution, available through most grocery or drug stores. By contrast, others are only available in exclusive department stores, product supply stores, online, or through "in the field" sales representatives who visit consumers in their homes (*e.g.*, Mary Kay, Avon). All of this is done with ease of access—or rather, convenience—for the customer in mind.

In higher education, the product "has usually been bound to geography—the physical location where a college or university does what it does" (Sevier 2003, p. 11). This may seem obvious: the "place" is the campus, where classes are held; however, there is a stronger, more impactful element to place, oftentimes correlated to convenience. In simple terms, how easy do colleges make it for students to "visit, attend and enroll" (p. 28). Generally, enrollment services directly affect the visitation, admission, and enrollment processes, while instructional units manage the where and when of classes and programs. However, an engaged SEM team allows for more comprehensive, campus-wide direction when it comes to making key place or convenience recommendations regarding how and where classes and services are delivered. The most obvious element is the physical location (*e.g.*, branch or satellite campuses and off-campus courses), but place also pertains to course modality (online, in-person, or hybrid) or times and days of offerings. Many institutions have traditionally been reluctant to expand offerings to late evening or weekend times, despite student demand. If part of the SEM direction includes meeting students' educational needs, then a SEM goal could be to expand where and when classes are offered. Non-credit programs (community education, adult basic education, and English language learning classes) comprise an excellent illustration of being responsive to consumer needs by offering classes throughout the day and week, via different modalities and locations—all done in an effort to better reach the customers in more convenient ways.

It is important that colleges not let themselves become stagnant in the traditional "place" element of its product. Colleges must continually monitor new strategies, as a variety of changes can affect student demand:

- Competitors could enter or leave the market (especially those from the proprietary sector).
- New modalities can be made available, especially through technology.
- Consumer demand can grow or wane.
- Area population demographics could influence program, course, or service offerings.

PROMOTION

In its most simplistic definition, SEM identifies the overall enrollment direction for an institution. When reviewing how SEM is intertwined with the four "Ps," one could easily draw an uncomplicated conclusion that the product equates to the institution's mission; price to tuition and fees; and place to the campus, its programs, and its services. While the reality is that each of these is much more complex, the fourth "P"—promotion—is fairly straightforward in concept, but the most complex to launch.

The terms "promotion" and "marketing" are often interchangeable. Regardless of which term is used, four primary components make up a promotion or marketing planning: marketing objectives, marketing audit, marketing strategies, and assessment.

In the business world, a *"marketing objective* is something that a marketing function is attempting to achieve in support of a strategic business plan" (Levens 2001, p. 26); the same holds true in education. Within SEM, the SEM goals become the marketing objectives. Examples will vary widely from institution to institution, but could include items such as increasing the yield rates from specific high schools, increasing the matriculation rate of students from ELL or ABE programs to credit programs, increasing the number of community education participants, or a multitude of other objectives.

Once goals are established, the next step is the *marketing audit*, which includes an evaluation of the internal and external forces that influence the objective, current initiatives associated with the objective, and the available talent and financial resources to support new directions.

The next step enters into the tangible details

TABLE 6.1

DEVELOPING A PROMOTIONAL PLAN

Goal	Target Market	Marketing Tactic
Increase the yield rates from high school "A"	15–18 year olds who attend high school "A"	Social networking, high school visit days, direct e-mail campaigns, movie theater advertisements
Increase the matriculation rate of adult basic education (ABE) students to credit programs	ABE students who complete advanced ABE classes	Classroom visits, individual appointments with admission counselors
Increase the number of community education participants	Middle income community members, ages 45–60	Newspaper advertisements, placement of community education schedule in select community locations

of the *marketing strategy*, or rather, how one intends to achieve its marketing goals. Within a marketing strategy comes the need to define the target market and the best tactics to reach it (*see* Table 6.1).

While the above is a simplistic illustration, it serves as a brief outline to developing a full promotional plan. Ultimately, a community college must go beyond trying the "one size fits all" approach to institutional promotional efforts and, instead, develop targeted messaging and communication plans for specific audiences and specific purposes. While doing so may seem daunting, a holistic approach such as this will supply a better return on staff and financial resources.

While the above examples are relatively tangible or concrete in nature, there is one aspect to promotion that is not so: the concept of public relations. Politicians are masters at using public relations—from having the perfect sound bite available whenever a reporter is near to making sure they are at any event that attracts a crowd and garners public access. Community colleges will also benefit from regular public relations efforts; this includes any effort to keep the college's name in the forefront of its constituents' minds. Examples include generic bulletin boards promoting the college's presence in the community; membership in area service clubs, which build connections to key members in the community; regular press releases touting staff or institution accomplishments; and participation or sponsorship of community events.

It is important for colleges to also remember that a mix of promotional opportunities is critical to the success of any campaign and that, more often than not, single-attempt or short-term campaigns do not provide long-term, strategic results. Nearly all admissions or college marketing directors can share stories of when someone in the campus leadership has asked for enrollment increases and wanted those increases by the start of the next academic term. An effective, comprehensive promotional plan will take at least two or more years to yield results. Therefore, promotion cannot be overlooked in the SEM planning process as promotion is the key to reaching many—if not all—SEM goals, including the recruitment and retention of students.

PEOPLE

While "people" do not constitute an official aspect of the marketing mix, they are a critical component of an effective SEM planning process. A statement from the opening section of this chapter is repeated for emphasis. That is, it takes the right people leading and advocating for a process that shapes the SEM plan in order to showcase important considerations in determining product, price, place, and promotion. A SEM plan—and by extension, the institution's product, price, place, and promotion—is successful only if the SEM planning team represents all facets of the institution.

While there is by no means an ideal make up to a SEM team, it is critical that it involves individuals who have connections with and are respected across the campus, as well as those who represent a variety of campus departments and are willing to spread the SEM "gospel" and, above all else, include members of the faculty. Obvious candidates for the SEM team are staff from admissions, records/registration, financial aid, and marketing, while other possible members are staff from institutional research, the college's foundation, noncredit learning, fiscal services/fiscal planning, academic advising, student life, and faculty from instructional leadership and specific academic divisions. The case study provided in the concluding chapter of this book talks in more detail about the development of an effective SEM team.

CONCLUSION

Ultimately, there are no immutable rules when it comes to the best approach to developing a SEM plan, nor to how an institution might employ the four "Ps" of the marketing mix. Regardless, both are critical to one another, and both provide unique opportunities for campuses to shed traditional boundaries, develop a dynamic team process, and, most importantly, have tremendous influence on its students' success.

7

SUPPORTING A SEM PLAN:
Role of Technology

by *Wendy* Kilgore *and* Kenneth Sharp

7 Much like the aphorism about personal computers becoming out-dated almost immediately upon purchase, the cutting-edge tech-nology discussed in this chapter may evolve and change even before publication. However, the basic tenets of this chapter will apply even as the technology evolves faster than practitioners can anticipate.

With that said, technology has become a necessary tool for SEM-related activity. It is required to deliver effective student services, as well as to provide actionable intelligence, such as the dashboard reports needed to inform decision-making. This need exists in a dynamic environment where the technologies we use are constantly evolving, as are the expectations of service from students, faculty, staff and other college stakeholders.

Often colleges think of technology only when there is a new product to buy or an existing technology fails to meet current needs. While this type of focus is appropriate at times, it does not offer a more holistic approach to technology. Colleges must also consider other aspects when examining the impact of technology on SEM efforts. Generally, the focus is on what technology is currently utilized by the college and what can be implemented to enhance SEM efforts. However, to ensure a comprehensive technology perspective, colleges should also make an allowance for the technologies being used by competitors, the technologies used by students (prospective, current, and former), and the technologies used by staff outside of their work environment.

Communicating effectively through technology with prospective and current students, many of whom are from the "wired generation," is often quite different from communicating similar content to prospective Generation X and other generations of students. The "wired generation" refers to those currently between the ages of sixteen and twenty-four who have been exposed to the internet since childhood (Barnes and Mattson 2009). The same generational differences will likely also exist for internal communication between offices and across generations of employees.

Critical components to consider when thinking about adopting or using technology for SEM efforts are the skill and comfort levels of staff towards technology and the amount of training and support needed for a successful implementation. When complaints are heard about the technology currently in use, is the situation a result of outmoded technology, insufficient staff training, or an unwillingness to use the technology among staff? In addition to understanding the skill level of those who use the technology, colleges must also be thoughtful when making decisions to change technology to improve or maintain SEM efforts. New technology often looks like it could revolutionize internal processes, but careful examination of this technology and how it will fit within the college is the only way to ensure an effective and successful SEM plan and technology integration. Although in most instances technology will enhance SEM efforts, it is not a foolproof solution. There exist possibilities for human error, incomplete adoption by staff, technology bridge limitations, limitations of the technology itself and others that can function as roadblocks to SEM efforts.

All of the issues briefly mentioned above should be part of the ongoing process of a college SEM plan. Adopting this inclusive technology perspective will help ensure that the technology in place or under consideration for implementation is an asset to the college's SEM efforts. These key issues and others are the focus of this chapter:

- An environmental scan of technology related to SEM efforts
- Importance of and how to measure technological competence of internal and external users
- Technology used in SEM efforts
- Technology roadblocks to SEM efforts
- Successful technology implementation

TECHNOLOGY AND A SEM ENVIRONMENT SCAN

External Scan

Periodic environmental scans provide the crucial constant feedback loop to help determine the effectiveness of certain SEM efforts and ensure their success. Practitioners might believe that an environmental scan could be something as simple as a student focus group regarding online admissions material, or as complex as a program review for an area of academic study. However, this internally-focused perspective discounts the potential impact of technologies external to the college on SEM efforts. Ideally, an external environmental scan should be a regular part of SEM efforts especially with recent technologies such as Twitter, Facebook, My Space, LinkedIn, and YouTube becoming so prevalent among college constituents. For the purposes of this chapter, constituents include both internal and external users of the technology, as well as prospective, current, and former students. These technologies, commonly referred to as Web 2.0, need to be understood as social technologies and include wikis, blogs, podcasts, RSS feeds, and others (Anderson 2007).

Recently Twitter has been in the news frequently. For those who may not be highly familiar with this new social networking site, it is a micro-blogging service that allows you to post anything you want in a text format of 140 characters or less, known as a Tweet. Similar to Facebook and MySpace, Twitter allows a user to sign in and view Tweets by other Twitter users and build a social network of Twitter users with either similar or dissimilar views. As practitioners, we might be quick to discount Twitter as having very little to nothing to do with SEM efforts. However, two recent examples highlight the impact Twitter can have on a person or an organization.

In the first case, a Twitter user named "theconner" posted what turned out to be a very public and quickly shared Tweet, *"Cisco just offered me a job! Now I have to weigh the utility of a fatty paycheck against the daily commute to San Jose and hating the work"* (Popkin 2009, p. 1). Shortly after, Tim Levad, a "channel partner advocate" for Cisco Alert posted the following response directed at "theconner," *"Who is the hiring manager. I'm sure they would love to know that you will hate the work. We here at Cisco are versed in the web"* (p. 2). By the end of the work day, news of the Tweet by "theconner" had spread quickly (*i.e.,* turned viral) through the Web. Consequently users were able to discern the real identity of "theconner" and posted it to the Web, earning "theconner" a new nickname and a Web page called "Ciscofatty" (www.ciscofatty.com) (Popkin 2009). It is unknown if the job offer to "theconner" was rescinded or whether she turned down the job before she posted the tweet. However, her Tweet remains an example of how something as simple as a post of 140 characters can have a negative impact on someone or a college.

The experience of Janis Krums, a passenger on a ferry in the Hudson on January 15, 2009, provides another example of the potential effect of a single Tweet. Krums posted the first photo of US Airways flight 1549 shortly after it landed in the Hudson River. Within thirty-four minutes of his post he was interviewed by MSNBC live as a witness to the event (Frommer 2009). Janis's Tweet was also viewed, shared, and posted by thousands of people in a very short period of time. Imagine the potential negative impact of a student posting a particularly viral negative and inflammatory Tweet about a college without the college's knowledge. On the other hand, what if something positive and equally viral was posted as a Tweet by college staff? This technology and others like it has the potential to reach large numbers of people in a very short period of time with small sound bites of information.

When selecting technologies for SEM efforts, consider their prevalence of use among target audiences. Between February 2008 and February 2009 Twitter usage grew a considerable 1,382 percent. Its user demographics will sound familiar to community college SEM practitioners (McGiboney 2009): for the four-week period ending January 17, 2009, 44.6 percent of Twitter users were between the ages of 25 and 34, 7.39 percent were 18 to 24 and an additional 14.04 percent were between the ages of 35 and 44 (Doughterty 2009). These cases clearly demonstrate the importance of scanning places like Twitter for college related comments. As an example, the edited comment below was found easily on Twitter in March of 2009:

They are all true **** major party school. Penny pitcher nights on Wed. 75 deg. weather in the winter, studying by pool in summer.

A recent cautionary tale about adopting Twitter and similar technology for SEM related efforts was posted on the Nielsen wire Web page: while the growth rate of users is extremely high for Twitter, 60 percent of those who sign up for Twitter abandon the service after a month (Martin 2009). Nielsen further noted that year-long retention rates of similar technologies including TweetDeck, TwitPic, Twitstat, Hootsuite, EasyTweets, Tumblr and others hovered around 30 percent. Before adopting new technologies like Twitter for SEM efforts, practitioners need to make sure it will be meaningful and useful to students; otherwise, they will not be return users, and over time the technology will lose its value to the college. A different way to approach quickly-evolving and easy-to-adopt technology is to make maximum use of the technology while it is popular, but remain ready to drop the technology and adopt others to replace it as new trends arise.

Monitoring the social networking sites and other Web 2.0 technologies for posts about the college should be an important part of SEM efforts. A 2007 National Association for College Admission Counseling (NACAC) research project reported that 53 percent (n=243) of the four-year colleges who participated in the survey stated that they monitor the internet for "*buzz, posts, conversations, and news about their institution*" (Nora Ganim Barnes 2007, p. 12). Even if we choose not to use Twitter and other related technologies in an active manner, we should at least passively look for negative and positive comments about our colleges since the potential exists for thousands of constituents to see the post. Practitioners could follow-up with those that post positive comments and possibly use the comments as quotes in recruitment materials. Cultivating the unsolicited positive comments is free marketing—building goodwill with those who are posting positive information and hopefully encouraging them to post more good things about the college. Addressing the negative comments through personal customer service could turn a detractor into a cheerleader for the institution.

Facebook, another rapidly growing social networking site frequently seen in the news, experienced a growth rate of 228 percent between February 2008 and February 2009 (Doughterty 2009). These explosive growth rates for Twitter, Facebook and other social networking technologies have led to the current concerns about social networking identity fraud and domain name infringement. For example, neither Facebook nor Twitter requires proof of a person's or organization's identity before assigning a profile name. Facebook does have a separate process for creating a page for a business or organization, but it simply asks the person to electronically certify their status as an official representative of the business or organization; no formal verification is required. A recent person search on Facebook resulted in three pages of Albert Einsteins, and an organization search found over five hundred matches for an institution with several advertising themselves as the "official" group for the college.

A component of Facebook that has seen an increase in users is the "fan pages" where someone can create a page for others to join as fans of that topic, organization, or interest. A recent fan page search on Facebook of a community college in the northwest turned up numerous fan pages (further chapter references to this college will use the pseudonym *Northwestern Community College)*. The content and layout of the fan pages do not indicate whether they are college sponsored or authorized. This means that an end user (prospective student) could view these sites and assume they are college sponsored and accurate. Identity fraud, or theft, and domain name infringement are such prevalent issues that for-profit services similar to Knowem.com, which search the use of a brand name on multiple social networking sites, are now widely available (Miller 2009).

While search engine technology is not new, it can also serve as a valuable tool in supporting a college's SEM efforts, particularly from the external scan perspective. Many will be familiar by now with the practice of using Google or other search engines to see what information surfaces as "hits" on the college name. However, practitioners are less likely to be familiar with the process of using Google and other search engines as tools for conducting external environmental scans. Ideally, the basic search utility should be used in combination with the recently enhanced Google Link functionality and similar resources. Unlike search engine logic that is driven by number of visits per page and relevance to key words, Google Link searches find Web sites that have direct links to a college's Web pages.

A recent Google Link search of Northwestern Community College's main Web page turned up about 30,100 direct links to this Web page from other Web sites. As expected with a number that large, not all of the links were from college sponsored sources. Some links were from college meta-search information pages and others contained legitimate links to the college. A number of the links associated with the college's domain name included misleading information about the college. For example, one link implying direct association with the college stated, "Is getting your Bachelors or Associates at Northwestern Community College right for you?" This particular community college does not offer bachelors degrees. This link also implied that all degrees were available online and in a self-paced format which is not correct. Other linked pages besides the one referenced above predominantly featured ads using the college's name, however, they were not sponsored by the college and in fact provided grossly erroneous information about the college.

Another Google Link search of a community college in the southwest found a direct link to a Web page featuring explicit adult material with simply the addition of the top level domain ".tf" to the college's main Web page. Top level domain refers to the right most part of the Web address. In this particular example the two-letter top level domain code refers specifically to a particular country or autonomous territory. The basic administrative information including contact information regarding the top level domain can be found using the Internet Assigned Numbers Authority "WhoIs" service (country-code top level domains).

The two Web pages described above were found using the advanced search Google Link function and represent about five minutes of search time. In October 2008, Google started offering a more advanced link-searching functionality through their webmaster tools, thus resulting in a more comprehensive data list that can be classified, filtered, and downloaded once verification of Web page ownership has been established.[2]

Colleges can employ a few methods to address the situations described above. These vary by the source of the infringement and misrepresentations. First, colleges can choose to address Web content in the same manner as if the information appeared in print. This includes pursuing legal action based on defamation, fraud, and trademark infringement, among others. If the content on the offending Web page is copyrighted and the Web page is hosted in the United States, a college can pursue legal action based on the Digital Millennium Copyright Act of 1998, which places an expectation on service providers to remove material from users' Web sites that appears to constitute copyright infringement.

More specifically related to domain name infringement, a college may use the following steps if the level of infringement is considered flagrant enough to warrant action:

- Find the owner and contact information for the Web site using one of the many "Whois" services available on the Web.

---

[2] *See* <http://googlewebmastercentral.blogspot.com/2007/02/discover-your-links.html>.

● Send a cease and desist letter to the owner of the Web site.
● Send a copy of the letter to the top-level domain registrar (this can also be found using Web searches).

Since domain infringement laws and rules vary by country, the efficacy of the above steps will depend somewhat on the country hosting the Web page and the country of origin for the top-level domain registrar. Finally, in situations where an individual or group has posted erroneous, defamatory, or fraudulent information through one of the social networking technologies, the simplest course of action is to register a complaint about the content of the Web page with the relevant service (*e.g.*, Facebook, Twitter, or MySpace) and then, contact the internet service provider hosting the Web page with the same complaint. Like domain infringement situations, the effectiveness of the steps above will vary by country (Worona 2009).

Practitioners can also use Google Alerts[3] to scan web content about their college. This free function allows you to sign up for e-mail updates of "the latest relevant Google results (Web, news, etc.) based on your choice of query or topic" (Google 2009). This functionality can be used not only to monitor the latest relevant results for your own college, but also to keep an eye on your competition.

Google is just one of many search engines used by potential students, their parents, and other stakeholders; the examples included above represent just a small sample of what can be found on the Web about colleges, accurate or not. Although it is not possible to control all uses of college domain names, this sort of external scan should still be conducted on a regular basis and attempts made to rectify the most egregious of the inaccuracies. A good percentage of prospective students will examine colleges through technology looking for the 'real culture' before visiting or attending colleges. As such it behooves practitioners to monitor those environments as part of SEM efforts.

All of the examples above represent what is currently cutting edge in Web 2.0 technology and social networking. It is impossible to manually scan all of these as well as other Web 2.0 technology like YouTube, LinkedIn (a professional social networking site), Flickr, Digg, and Delicious. This technology allows anyone with

---

[3] *See* <www.google.com/alerts>.

access to the internet to be a publisher. This fact, combined with the ability for Web users to create live feeds and updates on many of the social networking sites, makes regular monitoring of a college's image and Web presence worthwhile . Since staff time and expertise may be an issue with this process, companies like Nielson Online and several software packages can automate social network monitoring. Alternatively, Hubspot's Inbound Internet Marketing Blog offers the following advice on how to monitor college (or personal) social media presence in ten minutes a day (Corliss 2009):

- Check Twitter for chatter about your company: use tools like TweetDeck or Twitter Search to monitor conversations in real time.
- Set-up and scan Google Alerts.
- Check Facebook statistics: if your college has a Facebook page, view the page's insights.
- Answer industry/college-related LinkedIn questions.
- Use Google Reader to check Flickr, Delicious, Digg, and others.
- Set up RSS (really simple syndication) feeds for searches on your college name in other social media sites.

Many of these resources and techniques can be used to monitor a college's competition as well; it is equally valuable to know what the general public and/or internal constituents are saying about competitors.

Internal Scan

Scanning the internal technology environment of a college is no less important than scanning the external environment in support of SEM efforts. Internal scanning can be informal, for example inviting staff to let management know what they like and do not like about the technology used to support SEM efforts. Much can also be learned about internal technology by asking staff to map their business processes. An examination of these can reveal the manual processes in place because of insufficient knowledge about the technology or inadequate technology. Formally, technology usage scans track the time users spend with a particular technology down to as specific a detail as time spent on a particular task. However, this method requires a careful and thoughtful approach with clearly communicated goals shared with staff in advance of the monitoring, so as not to be perceived as a potentially punitive measure of work performance.

Existing policies and practices can both positively and negatively impact the effectiveness of technology relative to SEM efforts. For example, much of the system technology in place today is capable of instant admissions and registration, and therefore, amenable to the open enrollment generally offered by community colleges. That is, a prospective student can complete an online application, be evaluated by the system for potential existing student matches, and added to the system as a new or continuing student in a matter of a few seconds. The student can also receive an instant Web-based letter of admission providing them with a student ID and information on how to immediately log into the registration system. On the surface these seem like positive processes, but potential challenges must be considered. What if college policy requires a paper signature page (*i.e.*, not processed online) and, until the processing of this page, the student cannot register for classes? Will students fail to enroll because of this policy? While this policy may seem logical because colleges want to have a formal document indicating agreement to a student code of conduct, in this case the college is most likely losing students and revenue as a result of a) the policy of requiring a paper signature page instead of an electronic signature and b) the technology gap between the online application and the lack of an online signature option. As such, part of an internal scan should also include a review of business processes, practices, and procedures that might limit the use of technology in a college's SEM efforts. Finally you should examine your existing technology to determine the extent to which it is being used; in other words, is the technology in place and no one uses it, or is there room for improving SEM business practices in the software (*i.e.*, unrealized potential)?

This section has served as an introduction into the importance of internal and external scans of technology and its potential relevance to your SEM efforts. The next section will examine specific uses of technology in SEM efforts.

TECHNOLOGY AND SEM EFFORTS

There exists an abundance of software products marketed as ways to enhance and improve SEM efforts. These solutions vary from the simple add-ons, to common software designed to create professional letters and generate e-mails, to complex systems or suites designed to provide easy to access data for dashboards used to refine and inform SEM efforts. This section addresses the importance of understanding internal and external audiences' level of technology competence relative to SEM efforts, reflects on some common uses of technology in support of community college SEM efforts, highlights some additional solutions, and discusses common technology roadblocks to SEM efforts.

Measuring Technological Competence

Appropriate use of technology will increase the effectiveness of SEM efforts by increasing accessibility to the data used to drive decision making, improving usability for both internal and external users, and providing access to information in the manner most suitable to target audiences. One way to measure appropriateness is by assessing the ability of staff to use the technology and/or integrate the technology with existing processes to gain efficiencies. If staff are not trained to use the existing technology or brought into the process of selecting new technology, that product is not likely to be used to its full potential. Practitioners should regularly assess the information and communication technology (ICT) skill level of their staff. This skill assessment should not be delivered or mandated as a punitive action, but rather as a method for understanding in what areas staff needs additional training to become and maintain proficiency with the technology used in SEM efforts. Regular skill assessments and easy access to training result in increased staff satisfaction with their responsibilities and an increased use of the existing technology. Skill assessments also result in an easily-recognizable separation of deficiencies in technology from the need for additional staff training. There are many free and fee-for-service sources available to guide ICT skills assessment, and services vary from basic computer skills assessments to program specific training.

Staff familiarity with Web 2.0 technologies should also be assessed if the college is to adopt the use of or monitoring of these technologies in SEM efforts. A survey similar to one used by Dr. Nora Barnes, director of the University of Massachusetts Dartmouth Center for Marketing Research, is an uncomplicated way to gain an assessment of staff familiarity with Web 2.0 technologies. Dr. Barnes asked plainly, *"How familiar are you with the following...?"* and inserted the social networking technologies at the end of the question with the respondent choices including *"very familiar, somewhat familiar, somewhat unfamiliar or very unfamiliar"* (Barnes 2009). While 55 percent of the four-year college admissions department respondents in the 2007 NACAC study on social media reported that they were "very familiar" with social networking technology (Barnes 2009), the extent to which this holds true for community colleges is unclear. However, since community colleges are increasingly adopting the strategies and tools used by their four-year counterparts, this data may point to a future trend. A 2008 follow-up study by the same author found that 63 percent (n=536) of respondents reported being "very familiar" with social networking technology (Barnes and Mattson 2009).

It is obviously much more difficult to assess the ICT skills of an external audience (*i.e.*, prospective students, and others). However, staying current on trends in technology usage among constituent groups can guide decision-making regarding which technology to embrace for externally viewed SEM efforts. For example, when considering the use of interactive blogging or chat rooms in the recruiting and admissions process, an assessment of the target demographic use of this technology should precede adopting it as practice.

Recruiting and Admissions Technologies

"Recruitment efforts consist of communicating an institution's profile and culture in a variety of ways and in a logical progression" (Finnegan, Webb, and Morris 2007, p. 11). Practitioners are familiar with the traditional low-tech recruitment methods, such as high school visits, college fairs, targeted yield events, and others. While these practices remain in use, the advent of recent technological advances has introduced other ways for recruiters to reach potential students in support of the college's SEM efforts. For example, some colleges have begun using chat rooms in combination with targeted e-mails to specific demographic groups to create Web events where prospective students can join virtually with other prospective students and ask staff or current students questions about the college. A 2007 NACAC study including both two- and four-year colleges reported that colleges with an admission to enrollment yield of less than 30 percent were more likely to provide online chat opportunities as one method of attempting to increase yields (Finnegan, Webb, and Morris 2007). Increasingly community colleges are adopting constituent relationship management (CRM) solutions for their recruitment and SEM efforts. Among

other things, CRMs enable tailored messages to prospective students and the ability to track the communication for use in evaluating SEM efforts for particular target demographics. Social networking technologies such as blogs, Facebook, MySpace, and Twitter have also recently been added to the recruiter's technology tool box with mixed usage and relative effectiveness. For example, a recent *USA Today* article reported that the University of Minnesota football coach Tim Brewster uses Twitter to keep recruits and others interested in the athletic program (Marklein 2009). Additionally, 85 percent of the four-year colleges surveyed in 2008 reported that they used at least one form of social media, including blogs, message boards, podcasting, video blogging, and wikis (Barnes and Mattson 2009). As stated earlier, the extent to which this is true for community colleges is unclear, but this data may point to a future trend in community colleges.

Among two-year colleges 86.4 percent of those participating in the 2007 NACAC study on technology and admissions reported that they offered an online application (Finnegan, Webb, and Morris 2007). From the report it is unknown if the term online application referred to a fully online and integrated application or simply an application that could be completed online, but otherwise required printing and manual addition to the student database by staff. A fully automated online application for community colleges offers obvious advantages for an open door admissions practice. It enables the instantaneous admission of prospective students, including the assignment of a student ID and specific directions on how to register for classes. Depending on the college, this can be as simple as one mouse click away via a hyperlink in the online admissions letter that connects the student to the registration page. This automated response compliments the expectation of the "wired generation" for immediate action via the Web. It also enables colleges to spend much less staff time handling applications, thus freeing up time to quickly establish personalized contact with students, welcoming them to the college and informing them about orientation, financial aid, and other important information using a variety of technologies. Additionally, online applications enable a more rapid distribution of up-to-date information relative to SEM efforts, such as the dashboards used to drive strategic decision making.

Some colleges also use prospective student portals in their recruitment and admissions efforts. While portals can be rather static in their presentation and require a student to make the first contact with the institution, they also can be directly linked to dynamic college Facebook pages, which are much easier to update and link to other social networking technologies like Twitter. The combination of a prospective student portal and social networking technology greatly enhances a college's ability to remain dynamic and adjust to trends in what prospective students want to know and see about the college, as well as deliver the drier but no less important information about registration, billing, residential life, and financial aid.

POTENTIAL ROADBLOCKS

These new technologies have the potential to improve the recruitment services colleges provide to prospective students, as well as lower the costs of delivering services and increase the ability to use data to evaluate SEM efforts. Unfortunately, new technologies are not always able to deliver their full benefits to colleges. It is not unusual for a college to find upon purchasing a new technology that it is difficult to move data between the new system and older existing systems. The difficulties can result from incompatible data structures, a lack of information technology staff proficient with the specific technologies, or even an issue of timing feeds between systems, such as when data needs to be shared "real-time," but can only be fed on a nightly basis.

Additionally, not all new student contacts are made directly through recruiting related systems. No matter how sophisticated the recruitment related system, staff must still be able to enter data into the system. Administrative interfaces are not always as intuitive to use as the client interfaces. Further, they may be designed to accommodate many simultaneous users, but not to accommodate a single user making multiple entries.

Moreover, technologies used in student recruitment can require that prospective students complete all the information or data fields necessary to develop a prospect record. Students recruited or expressing interest in a college utilizing a non-technological solution may not provide all the information required for a successful recruitment/prospect contact. In cases like this, the format of the data may not be compatible with the prospecting system or may be incomplete, but still processed into the recruitment system. These limitations in the data and the technology may result in a mismatch of data between the recruitment information and the applicant information for the same student.

Matching records between prospects and admissions applications or admissions represents perhaps the largest challenge associated with recruitment and prospecting technologies. This challenge generates two primary problems: the creation of duplicate records; and, as a result, difficulty in evaluating the efficacy of recruiting activities. Duplicate records potentially lead to several problems for the prospective student and the college. As an example, an admitted student could continue to receive recruitment contacts, thus possibly reducing the student's perception of the credibility of the college. Or, portions of the student's record could be matched up with different recruitment records (*e.g.*, some from a FAFSA feed with some from a recruitment contact). Detecting and resolving duplicate records can be time consuming and damaging to the prospect's relationship to the college. Duplicate records also lead to difficulties assessing the efficacy of recruiting activities and SEM efforts. Multiple records foster the impression that the college has a greater number of recruits/prospects than have actually been generated. The result can be a misstatement of the cost effectiveness of recruiting and can translate to lower yield rates than expected.

Complications may also arise when applying new technologies to the admissions process. For example, the product's accessibility can affect both the perspective of student access to the technology and the usability of the product. Community college students tend to be older than their four-year counterparts and may have limited access to, or ability to use, computer-based technologies. Additionally, a cultural paradigm has developed creating an expectation that technologies will be available seven days a week on a twenty-four hour basis. Colleges may not have the capability or staffing to ensure the availability of admissions technology to meet this expectation.

The ability to communicate quickly with a large number of students at once constitutes another issue with both positive and negative aspects. While this technology increases efficiencies by allowing for e-mail contact with hundreds of students simultaneously, it also enables large scale mistakes that would normally not occur with printed materials such as admissions letters. A recent quote from an AACRAO official in the *San Diego Union-Tribune* summed up these errors well with, "...the advent of automated systems means that potentially you could put any mistake on steroids.... In the old days, maybe it was one letter going in the wrong envelope.

Now you push the wrong button and thousands of people get the wrong message" (Wilkens 2009, p. 1).

Additionally, many admissions-related technologies are based on the four-year college paradigm. Community colleges practitioners may find that "out of the box" limitations on technologies may require administrative work-arounds, modifications to the technology, or a redefinition of the data fields used in the application. In one instance, the use of general level degree listings in the application for admission for non-technical associate degrees and certificates (*e.g.,* associate of arts, associate of science and associate of general studies) does not allow for intuitive links between a student's interest in biology, for example, and the associate of science degree. This constraint of some enterprise resource planning (ERP) products leads to confusion on the admission application because prospective students see only the general degree listings and not what they understand as "majors" based on the four-year model. However, when this same technology is used by a four-year institution with majors in the traditional sense, the ERP lists those majors as the available paths of study on the Web application without any modifications. Lastly, as with recruiting, matching student records between recruiting systems and admissions systems is critical.

Pre-Enrollment and Enrollment Technologies

Fewer than three-quarters of the two-year colleges participating in the 2007 NACAC report on admissions technology reported using an online course registration system. Although this may seem like a lower percentage than expected, it was based on 2005 data. In addition, usage was significantly higher than the four-year counterparts with 57.4 percent online registration availability (Finnegan, Webb, and Morris 2007). Relatively new to the pre-enrollment and enrollment technology toolkit are the ability to offer virtual advising, chat room advising, and online assessments of college readiness which communicate scores directly into the course registration system and allow students to register for the appropriate classes. All of these technologies enhance the ability of students to help themselves without needing college staff to move forward in the enrollment process. By augmenting pre-enrollment and enrollment services through technology, the colleges free up staff time to focus on the students who need the hands-on help. This has the potential to increase the retention rates of both populations of students: those who can and do want to help themselves and those who need and will receive help.

POTENTIAL ROADBLOCKS

These technologies provide many opportunities to enhance the services colleges provide to students and possess the potential to increase the hours a college's services are available to students. However, when the college provides enhanced services and increases the hours that services are available, students have an expectation that services will match those provided elsewhere, particularly on the Internet. They expect shopping cart simplicity in the applications they access and around the clock availability with no system down-time. Sometimes policy/practice can conflict with the enhancements available through technology and potentially backfire on SEM efforts. For example, although community colleges generally maintain an open door admissions policy, some require an application fee by policy or practice. If the fee payment technology lacks the functionality needed to integrate with the admissions and enrollment technology, an advance payment would be required from students who would otherwise be instantly admitted or paying for classes on the spot. This mismatch of technology and practice is contrary to students' regular interactions with Web vendors such as Amazon.com. Policy and practice should also be regularly reviewed as complementary technology advances and is adopted. Failure to do so may lead to practices and policies that result in students turning away from the college because the technology does not reflect what they are used to as Web customers.

A frequently ignored constraint on enrollment related technologies is the size of the "data pipes" or bandwidth available to a college, particularly in rural areas. Unless specific policies are in place, many community college students have a tendency to delay registration until the drop/add period or will "shop" classes, dropping and adding courses until they find an acceptable combination. This drop/add activity can coincide with late student applications and students trying to access online classes, thus instigating a data "traffic jam" and significantly slowing system response times or even causing failures in critical systems.

Another issue that can arise is the synchronization of critical systems during this period of frenzied activity. As students enroll in online classes, they expect to be able to instantly access their class. To try and circumvent this problem, in many cases, system constraints dictate the movement of information between the college's ERP and the college's CMS on a nightly basis to preserve system resources for enrollment activity.

Retention Technologies

Where it is adopted, portal technology is regularly used to support retention and SEM efforts both from the student perspective and internal staff perspective. For example, the portal can be used in combination with data extraction scripts to automatically generate personal e-mails or targeted announcements for students who have received a poor midterm grade. Some colleges also combine one-click services through the online course management system, enabling faculty members to send announcements straight to a particular group of students regarding a change in schedule or assignment reminder, or even to one student about a missing project. This one-click technology for faculty can also be tied to automated workflows, whereby an online trigger from a faculty member regarding a student's multiple absences will send a message to the student's advisor and, if applicable, the financial aid office and the veteran's educational benefits liaison. Each of these automated contacts would then prompt other staff to also touch base with the student.

Automated workflows can also be created to deliver e-mails when a registration action is taken by a student. For example, a workflow can be implemented that triggers action when a financial aid student drops a course, changing his financial aid eligibility from full-time to part-time. Again, this can be set up to send an e-mail or even a text message to the student and a workflow notification to the financial aid office and advising office. Similarly, a workflow could let faculty know when a student has completed a make-up assignment or test in the testing center. The possible uses of this technology are many and range from very simple to highly complex processes.

Administrators can also take advantage of the portal technologies in the monitoring of SEM efforts. Data for an enrollment-related dashboard can be collected and formatted in either an add-on enrollment solution or managed in-house and sent to particular administrators via the portal with targeted announcements or a dedicated channel visible on the primary administrative portal tab. This leaves the data at the fingertips of administrators who want to be kept up to date on key performance indicators.

These technologies and others like them tend to increase retention because of their high student touch factor. Not only are college staff and faculty interacting with them in person (or possibly entirely online) in the classroom setting, but the college is reaching out to them through these other methods and tying multi-modal learning methods into the retention practices.

POTENTIAL ROADBLOCKS

Although technology frequently appears ubiquitous and easy to use, this is not always the case. The technology itself, its usability, and the expectations surrounding it can influence student retention. For example, many colleges establish student e-mail systems and supporting policy with the intent of using them as the primary method of communication with students. Unfortunately, not all students participate in college e-mail systems, even with the threat of punitive action for lack of participation. Some of the issues observed include, students who do not seem to understand the significance of the e-mail system as the primary method of communication between the student and college; students who keep checking their home e-mail system (*e.g.*, gmail, hotmail, etc.) without understanding that their college e-mail is not automatically forwarded; and students who prefer not to use e-mail. In any of these cases, when a college chooses to communicate only through e-mail or through a portal, the potential exists to lose the student as a result of a lack of communication. The same applies to administrative staff; if the key performance indicators are posted on a dedicated portal channel, but the administrators do not use the portal to regularly access other work-related solutions like e-mail and calendaring, there is very little to drive the administrator to open the portal on a regular basis.

The implementation of new technologies should be accompanied by the encouragement of faculty and staff to take advantage of them. Not all faculty and staff, however, are ready to use technology with the same level of competence and adoption rate. Some individuals may be resistant to change, some may fear technology, others may just be modern day Luddites who see technology as a threat to their way of life, or they may be "CAVE people" (Colleagues Against Virtually Everything). No matter how intuitive and helpful a technology, their first instinct will be to reject it.

FIGURE 7.1 ▶

Sample student intent
modification to ERP

SOURCE: REPRINTED
WITH PERMISSION FROM
A COMMUNITY COLLEGE
IN THE SOUTHWEST

Student Intent

The first time you register each semester, you will be asked the questions below. Answering these questions will assist in delivering services customized to your educational goal/major. Please complete the questionnaire, click submit, and continue on with the registration process.

Please verify your address and phone number. To update your records, click here.

NAME	[First] [Last]
ADDRESS	[Street Address]
PHONE NUMBER	[XXX-XXX-XXXX]
SELECT REASON FOR ATTENDING [UNIVERSITY X]	O Pursuing a(n) [X] degree or certificate O Taking courses for transfer to a 4-year college/university O Taking courses for personal interest O Taking courses for job skills O University [X] student taking courses at [University Y]
DO YOU PLAN TO RETURN TO [UNIVERSITY X] NEXT:	*Summer 2009* ⊙ Yes O No *Fall 2009* ⊙ Yes O No
IF NO, PLEASE SELECT YOUR PRIMARY REASON:	O Completed program of study O Achieved educational goal O Transfer to a 4-year college/university O Change in employment O Relocation O Military deployment O Course(s) not available O Financial reasons O Family/personal reasons O Other; tell us why:
YOUR EDUCATIONAL GOAL/MAJOR IS:	Liberal Arts (Agec-A)-AA

Lastly, there are technological limits to understanding why students leave. When students choose to leave college, it is much easier for them to cease logging into a course management system or the college e-mail system than it is to tell an instructor or advisor that they are dropping out of college. Additionally, there are not many technological solutions to assist colleges in determining and tracking the reasons students leave the college. As an example, did the student leave because he/she completed the classes needed for a job, or did he/she drop out, failing to complete a degree or certificate program? Observationally, many community college students select a degree as their program of study simply to qualify for financial aid.

Colleges will count these students as non-completers if they leave the college before fulfilling the degree requirements. Some community colleges have either developed or purchased an interface that captures student intent on a term-by-term basis (*See* Figure 7.1). Data collected, either through online registrations or in-person registrations, enables the college to more accurately detail a student's intent, and provides the college with useful information for measuring the effectiveness of select SEM efforts. The data can also be used to enhance the accuracy of course scheduling if used in combination with a degree audit system.

Degree Completion Technologies

Degree audit systems are probably the most common technology associated with degree completion. The most sophisticated of the degree audits use Web-based interfaces for both staff and students. They enable a student to monitor progress towards completion of her academic goal in an easy-to-read format. These technologies also provide the student the opportunity to assess their own process toward a degree or certificate and run their own "what-if" scenarios to see what coursework would be required to obtain an additional degree or certificate. Practitioners may wonder how this particular type of technology can be used to support SEM efforts. In its most rudimentary functionality, the technology provides a clear academic path for students to follow while at the institution—as compared to paper check-sheets and other non-automated processes—thus improving the likelihood of students reaching their education goal. Similar to the earlier stated information about registration technology, degree audit systems also free staff time for those students who really need the additional one-on-one help and remove restrictions of time and location on service to students.

Students can use degree audit systems in educational planning across multiple terms, and this information can then be used by the college to plan course offerings. This aspect of the technology supports SEM by increasing the likelihood that a needed course is in the course schedule for a particular term, a particularly important factor for capstone courses or other specialized courses required for certain degrees and certificates. If the college is not aware that a cohort of forty-five students is going to need the specialized course next term and only offers one section, the likelihood of losing degree completers rises. Students will often not wait another semester to take a course, either because they are not able to wait or lose interest. Since community college success is still most often measured by degree completers, the ability for a college to use technology to support degree completion should be closely tied to SEM efforts.

Depending on a college's graduation application practices, the degree audit system has the capacity to run batch analyses of students within a certain number of credit hours of their educational goal. This data is then used to send targeted messages to the students encouraging them towards degree completion and reminding them of the application process. Similarly, for those students who have failed to return after successful enrollment but no degree completion, degree audit analyses can inform targeted marketing material to encourage those students close to reaching their academic goal to return to college. Perhaps controversially, colleges can also use this technology to award degrees to students who failed to apply for or complete a technical degree (AAS), but meet the degree requirements for a non-technical degree like an associate of general studies. The purpose of this practice is twofold: the student would probably be happy to receive a degree and may be encouraged to continue his education, and the college receives credit for degree completion. Finally, colleges can also use this technology to encourage students who are simply pursuing a certificate to continue towards a degree by letting the student know they might only need a few more credit hours to complete a degree.

POTENTIAL ROADBLOCKS

Just as there have been roadblocks associated with the technologies used for recruiting, admitting, enrolling, and retaining students, roadblocks also occur in the process of helping students successfully exit college. A basic paradigm in higher education has been to require students to apply for their degree in order to graduate. Current technologies provide the opportunity for colleges to learn which students are able to graduate based on their academic history and even to suggest other degrees or certificates the student would be eligible for with additional course work. However, maintaining a degree audit system with these capabilities is staff intensive. Community colleges change programs and program content frequently, requiring constant updating of degree audit systems. Additionally, degree audit systems require increased communication between faculty and the registrar's office. Timely communications of degree substitutions becomes critical, as does consistency in the types of substitutions provided.

SUCCESSFUL SELECTION AND IMPLEMENTATION OF TECHNOLOGY

Given the realities described in this chapter, decisions to update or enhance current SEM-related technology, or to implement new technology, are inherently part of a college's success. In fact, ERP systems, and their associated issues of cost, staff development, user training, business process modifications, and regulatory compliance were chosen as number two in importance for the strategic success of colleges among the issues ranked by information technology leaders for 2008 (Allison 2008).

When existing technology no longer enables the college to meet its needs or to keep up with its peers, the implementation of new SEM-related technology must take place. However, the idea of implementing new technology, either an entirely new ERP or add-on SEM-related solutions, can be perceived by staff as a daunting and unpleasant task. This is especially true for those who are not part of the information technology unit or who currently use technology strictly as a tool to complete clerical functions. Even when staff supports the change in technology, finding time to complete the required steps, while keeping up with ongoing workload, is a major challenge.

In order to be successful, any technology implementation must be carefully planned to minimize any perceived negative impact on staff and/or daily operations. Successful implementation of enrollment-related technology hinges on factors similar to managing any significant organizational change, such as a clear vision of the end goals, a champion for the effort, systemic buy-in from cross functional areas, and the development of a realistic timeline.

Phelps and Busby (2007) describe implementing a new system as similar to remodeling a house in that there are typical questions such as, "Where can you upgrade or make things easier" or "Why not put in new plumbing and electrical systems since you have already ripped down the walls?" Before making a SEM-related technology purchase, questions like those listed below should be thoughtfully addressed.

- What is our budget for purchase, implementation, support, and maintenance?
- What functional areas are going to be impacted by this change in technology (*e.g.*, admissions, records, registration, institutional research, finance)?

- What business processes are we trying to change and improve with this new technology and why? What other business processes will be affected?
- Do our current processes need to be reviewed for relevance to the end goal and the new technology?
- What is our customization expectation?
- How much training is needed for staff to use the new technology?
- Will we be able to extract the data we need from the technology for our operational and regulatory purposes?
- What is the timeline for the implementation, and does that timeline conflict with operational business cycles?

Once a college has addressed the questions listed above and selected a SEM-related technology, there are seven additional questions that are critical not only to a successful implementation, but also to a college's overall enrollment efforts (Nah and Delgado 2006). These questions include:

- How will this technology enhance the college's ability to fulfill its strategic plan?
- Is the college's level of preparedness for the operational and cultural changes that will result from the implementation adequate?
- Is there a clear communication plan regarding the implementation with all stakeholders?
- Are those involved in the details representative of all of the business areas impacted by the new technology?
- Are the college's governance structures supportive of the change, and is the team leadership for the project given an appropriate level of authority and responsibility to get the job done?
- Is there a clearly defined scope and timeline for the project?
- Is there adequate technical expertise (both in the operational unit and in the information technology unit) and infrastructure to support the new technology?

POST-IMPLEMENTATION CONSIDERATIONS

Throughout the implementation phase, the focus is primarily on "going live," however, "going live' is not the end of implementation. As in any planning process, the next step should focus on improving the deployment. This can include, examining functionality that was not initially implemented; re-examining perceptions that drove the initial implementation decisions; re-examining the college's business processes and business paradigms; and sharing and collaborating with other colleges who have previously implemented similar systems.

The environment of higher education is constantly changing as a result of both internal and external factors and changes in technology. As a result, the improvement process is not limited to the period immediately following implementation, but really represents a continuous cycle of activity. As such, successful SEM-related technology implementation will continue to be best served by using a holistic approach from the selection of a product to the end of its lifecycle.

CONCLUSION

This chapter was designed to provide SEM practitioners with an overview of the issues and opportunities associated with the technologies that may influence their SEM efforts. As practitioners, it is not unusual to focus on the benefits promised by new technologies or to only focus on the technologies controlled within the college. However, to use technologies to the best advantage, efforts must be focused both internally and externally. Internally, colleges must first understand how students, staff, and faculty interact with the college's SEM technologies; then, either accept both the staff and technology limitations by developing practices to accommodate these limitations or take an active role in facilitating positive, meaningful interactions by improving staff ICT skills or improving the technology. Finally, it is also important for the college to have an awareness of the external technologies that prospective and current students are actively engaged with and how they may influence SEM efforts.

DEVELOPING AND IMPLEMENTING A STUDENT
Recruitment Plan

by Bruce Clemetsen *and* Dennis Bailey-Fougnier

8

"Strategic Enrollment Management (SEM) is more than simply beef-
ing up recruitment, creating a one-stop center, or counseling at risk-
students" (Kerlin 2008). While student recruitment is an important
component of a SEM plan, it should not be the sole focus, or even
necessarily the main one. To achieve optimum enrollment requires consideration of
retention as well as recruitment. The authors, from experience, would further note
that any community college implementing a SEM plan would be well advised to
initially focus on retention and student success, as the information acquired about
students and programs will create an excellent foundation for developing a recruitment strategy and the resultant plan.

Nonetheless, we reiterate that student recruitment does constitute an important
component of a SEM plan. Thus, in this chapter, we break the broader SEM rule and
focus on recruitment. As with all of SEM, recruitment in community colleges is a
recent phenomenon, emerging largely in the last ten to fifteen years in response to
environmental forces described in the introduction of this book. A search revealed
virtually no professional literature on the evolution of recruitment in the community college setting. This is not reflective of the innovative recruitment work being
done at two-year institutions in the U.S., Canada, and abroad, but does speak to the
newness of the concept and the lag time between practice and its documentation
in professional media (aside from conference presentations and localized publications). Thus, the assertions of this chapter are drawn from the experiences of the authors, sharing information that colleagues have found helpful and models to review
as reference material to guide development of recruitment efforts at community

colleges. Our intent is to stimulate further dialogue, experimentation, and professional writing.

EVOLUTION OF COMMUNITY COLLEGE RECRUITMENT

Community colleges were established to meet local community access needs to postsecondary education. Student recruitment has evolved with the maturation of community colleges and their communities. Before addressing recruitment issues related to the present and future, it is important to contemplate why recruitment has become important for community colleges. To this end, the following chronology is used to account for the evolution of the recruitment function at community colleges:

1. Build it and they will come
2. Everyone knows your name
3. Moving from passive to active recruitment
4. Recruitment as a recognized organizational function
5. Recruitment guided by Strategic Enrollment Management

Community colleges have been moving through this evolution as a result of competitive pressures, changes to funding formulas, expanding missions, and rising public expectations. Not all community colleges will have experienced these phases of recruitment models; however, we hope they explain past and current situations, giving context to why certain conditions exist and what might be needed to move to the next phase.

The initial recruitment model implemented by community colleges tended to be built on the philosophy of "build it and they will come." The rationale for this was based on the community voting to create or lobbying the state legislature for the construction of a community college in their municipality. The level of support, among other factors, contributed to the decision making process. The need for organizational structure and systems to support recruitment was not necessary—the evidence demonstrated by the historical enrollment numbers of the early years of most community colleges. This model began to change as local populations grew and the founders moved away from being involved in the creation of a community college.

The next recruitment model to emerge was the "everyone knows your name" approach. Though not so new, community colleges remained highly connected to changing community needs. Institutional missions and programs were impacted by the changing workforce and educational needs of their service districts. For those institutions funded through periodic property tax levies or other local tax approvals, the need to stay connected to tax payers was especially strong and ensured that the community was constantly reminded about the success, value, and open door to the local community college. This active engagement with every household in the service area kept the college, its programs, and availability as an educational resource at the forefront of many who sought local, affordable higher education.

Community colleges matured and began to be impacted by changing demographics, growing college attendance, growing competition, and changes in funding mechanisms. The impact of these forces compelled community colleges to begin to rely on some level of outreach to attract students. More diverse prospective student markets became important for meeting colleges' access mission. These new markets required more relationship building and support in order to bring them through the door of the community college. With community interest in postsecondary education growing, communicating with prospective students without expecting them to come to campus became an important service. Changes in business and industry led to the replacement of academic programs. Some states moved community colleges to a majority state funding formula from the initial local formula. This move, where it occurred, changed colleges' relationship with their local community. The loss of regular contact and information sharing that local bond levy campaigning provided had to be replaced by other methods of connecting with the community. Additionally, competition from new and expanding entrants into higher education created competition in local markets. These forces disconnected colleges from their communities. To counter these changes required colleges to begin sending people, usually counselors and others who knew the college well, into the community to inform prospective students about the college's programs and enrollment processes.

From an internet search, it is clear that many community colleges have developed, or are developing active recruitment programs. Resources dedicated to outreach and recruitment reflect a move to create an improved structure for building new relationships with the community to help people connect with the myriad of educational opportunities offered. This growing structure supports a continued commitment to access. As funding formulae and stakeholders have placed value on growth and various market penetrations, the recruitment program has been revealed as fundamental to institutional health. The growth of communication technology has added to the need for organized efforts to build connections with prospective students in the community. A strategic approach to recruitment and outreach, supported with sufficient resources, effectively builds paths to facilitate enrollment growth from existing and new markets. Those outcomes provide evidence of continued success in meeting our access mission.

With the growing adaptation of SEM concepts to the community college setting, recruitment is a function that is quickly reviewed for its strategy and effectiveness in meeting institutional goals. With changes in accountability, recognition of the cost of recruiting versus retaining a student, and significant attention to student success, being more intentional in recruitment efforts has become a necessity. The paradox for community college recruitment and SEM leaders is that growth and access remain paramount in our mission and metric, but so do student retention, progress through educational levels, and completion. In the strategic phase, the strategic plan and the academic master plan guide recruitment. These plans provide the critical direction for understanding the multitude of markets for the diverse academic programs contained within the institution. A crucial awareness of program cost per student ensures that sufficient students are brought into low cost programs, to support high cost programs. The definition of "community" is expanding as institutions offer programs to meet regional employment needs.

DEVELOPING A RECRUITMENT PLAN

Whether a community college is at capacity or needs to fill its classrooms, every college needs to develop an effective student recruitment plan. Since their inception, most community colleges bought into the "build it and they will come" type of recruitment. Community colleges have long sent counselors out to district high schools, mostly to help students enroll in classes. They generally have not cultivated new prospective students; most have not had to. In fact, a good number of community colleges do not even have an official outreach office. However, the viability of such an approach to recruitment is a relic of the past for most colleges. A well-constructed student recruitment plan will, at least, help community colleges meet their missions by reaching out to at-risk students: low-income, first-generation, returning adults, underrepresented student of all kinds.

A strategic recruitment plan must reach many parts of the campus in order to encompass diverse missions. Described below are several steps towards developing a plan. There is a certain logic to the order of the elements described below, though it is likely that they may happen simultaneously and may not follow a linear pattern.

Relating Recruitment to the Strategic Plan and Academic Master Plan

The strategic plan and the academic master plan, together, offer the enrollment manager direction for where the community college intends to grow. The change and growth, whether explicit or implied, in these plans guides the quantity, educational goals, and community markets targeted in order to support the planned growth. Teasing out the student markets and student demographic characteristics is done in conjunction with the creation of the plans. However, most likely a SEM team will need to review the planning documents and meet with key stakeholders to illuminate the desired student market.

Collecting Critical Data to Shape the Plan

Before embarking on marketing and outreach efforts to attract students that will support strategic plans or fulfill academic development plans, enrollment managers need to review information about the students and programs in existence at the institution. Developing a recruitment plan requires an understanding of current student pathways to the institution and programs. Additionally, some information about what current influences support students finding the pathway and making the connection with the community college will assist in devising the plan. Finally, the recruitment plan must be built around an understanding of the cost per student for various programs. These factors guide the shaping of the plan based on current strengths and knowledge of student markets and programs.

One does not have to develop highly sophisticated tracking systems to begin understanding the demographic coming to the community college. Several existing sources of data can supply a student's origins. Institutions can mine data from the FAFSA, ACT, and/or SAT information received, demographic questions on placement tests, admission applications, state reporting forms, and other existing sources. These are often rich in information about where students were prior to attending college. With the growing numbers of transfers and reverse transfers, the National Student Clearinghouse's Student Search Service can reveal from and to where these groups are transferring. Another similar approach involves reviewing counts of received transcripts and entering student majors. Also, a look at students' funding sources can show which students are coming through particular employers or community agencies.

Identifying high schools, agencies, universities, and the programs of entry provides a picture of existing paths and potentially important relationships for a recruitment plan. The strength of relationships that support people to seek education and specifically encourage people to consider your community college is a valuable asset to build into a recruitment plan. Be prepared to also learn where students do not come from, revealing a lack of strong support relationships which, if needed to support strategic plans or program goals, will require an investment to improve. Having a solid understanding of people and organizations supporting recruitment efforts from outside the institution is helpful in planning, resources allocation, and offers great opportunity for new efforts.

Knowing program costs and program capacity comprises critical data for a strategic recruitment plan. SEM is intrinsically tied to managing enrollments in relation to resources. Certain programs cost more per student than others. Recruitment plans must be sensitive to directing sufficient enrollments into low-cost programs so as to offset enrollments into high-cost programs. In addition, some types of students cost more to recruit and to support at the community college. Care should be made to balance enrollments with support services provided in order to produce sufficient levels of student success for all students in all programs.

Finding Supportive Allies

Recruitment is a complex process that brings together a variety of institutional stakeholders for the purpose of supporting the vision and goals of the institution. A recruitment plan requires support from a variety of internal and external audiences including the president, senior administrators, faculty, staff, alumni, board of trustees, and current students. "To engender 'buy-in,' engage as many different individuals in the planning process as reasonably possible by soliciting their feedback and participation" (Papa 2002, p. 6). At most colleges there are plenty of faculty already conducting recruiting, especially in certificate programs of one year or less or with cohort based programs that rely on enough students at the entry point to make the program viable. There will be others who understand the need to reach into the community and connect with people about the opportunities at the community college. Capitalize on the motivations of these individuals to advance the need for planning and coordination of recruitment efforts.

Determining Institutional Strengths

Putting the community college's "best foot forward" is important in establishing the reasons for community members to enroll. A recruitment plan reflects the programmatic and cultural strengths of the community college. This information guides marketing and advertising. It also provides a partial explanation for the current student profile, revealing why current practices may be successful or unsuccessful in meeting the institution's optimum enrollment level and mix.

Finding institutional strengths involves a number of approaches to assessment. Some colleges conduct surveys of incoming students to determine why they made the choice to attend. This provides rich information about what students see as attractive institutional factors. Data benchmarked against other similar institutions and competitors offers direct comparative information about institutional strengths. Interviewing external groups—high school counselors, work force counselors, business owners, and community leaders—can be very revealing about the institution's strengths from those who may encourage prospective students to enroll.

Determining Competition for Market Niches and Programs

A recruitment plan is not developed in a vacuum; hence, it is important to consider the impact of competition. Today there are more options for all the types of programs that exist in community colleges—language institutes, career colleges, GED programs, online options—creating the necessity for understanding institutional strengths in relation to what competitors offer. An awareness of the options available to the community and the factors that influence students' decisions to attend the community college versus another educational provider will shape recruitment goals and activities. Talking with faculty about variables that distinguish their individual programs from others, what they see as successful entering student characteristics, and job demand and placement exposes their important insights into how much competition exists for prospective students and graduates.

Scanning for New Opportunities

In addition to determining competition, the development of a recruitment plan should be informed by opportunities to attract new populations, underserved segments of the community, and untapped markets. Changing demographics, economic factors, potential partnerships, academic programs, and delivery methods provide opportunities to be accounted for in a community college recruitment plan. New opportunities may come from grants that enable the design of improved support and academic preparation programs for underserved populations or the creation of a program with local high schools to recruit students who do not complete a diploma, but who are capable of college level work. Another approach is actively learning about talent shortages being experienced by staffing companies. This information can lead to new programs or reflect demand for existing program graduates. It can also be translated into recruitment efforts that connect prospective students to a clear path to employment. Other opportunities arise when a university designs a new degree program, creating the opportunity for community college faculty to negotiate the articulation of existing or new courses that support the baccalaureate program. In this case, both institutions gain from the cooperative promotion and recruitment effort.

Setting Targets

Having goals for recruitment efforts foments energy and direction for new efforts, as well as the benchmarking of established recruitment efforts. For new initiatives, the staff charged with implementation needs a target to strive for so that sufficient resources are focused, milestones can be set, and success visible. Targets ought to be clearly articulated to the related parts of the strategic plan or the academic master plan. The clearer the target and its relationship to institutional direction, the more likely the recruitment effort gains the resources needed for successful implementation.

One vital resource for efforts specifically tied to academic master plan element is the engagement of the affected faculty and instructional leadership. Having clear targets makes apparent to these allies the value of their involvement. Including faculty in setting recruitment targets involves them in the process of market assessment and communications, capacity determination, program quality features, and acknowledges the joint responsibility for success.

Feedback Loops

Finally, a recruitment plan requires regular review and renewal so that enrollment goals align with community and institutional changes. Establishing feedback loops that bring information to the plan from internal and external constituents keeps the plan current and viable. External contacts can describe the competitive environment, highlight institutional strengths, expose changing demographic trends, and provide alerts as to how well the institution informs constituents about programs and processes. Internal constituents provide important feedback on whether enrollment levels and student composition make good matches for meeting retention and completion goals. Developing some routine assessments of the recruitment plan that include quantitative targets, but also qualitative information from those who are "ambassadors" of the community college in the community is critical to having a quality recruitment program.

CORE RECRUITMENT PRACTICES

There are several core practices that enrollment managers should consider when implementing a recruitment effort; the following serve to guide recruitment planning and effectively build relationships with prospective students:

- The Enrollment Funnel
- Inquiry Generation
- Communication Plan

Each of these core practices are described below. The authors have found these practices to be helpful in improving recruitment efforts and for setting goals for recruitment program development.

The Enrollment Funnel

Before developing a student recruitment plan, one needs to understand where currently enrolled students came from and how many potential students it takes to reach the college's optimum enrollment.

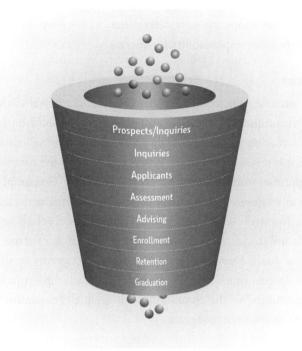

FIGURE 8.1 ▶

Community College
Enrollment Funnel

Prospects/Inquiries

Inquiries

Applicants

Assessment

Advising

Enrollment

Retention

Graduation

Recruitment has traditionally subscribed to the funnel model, which is altered slightly here to reflect the unique circumstances of the community college setting.

The funnel represents the recruiting cycle of potential students to the students who actually begin classes at your institution. Community colleges have paid very little attention to the recruitment-to-enrollment process. Many have little idea where their students really come from or how the students found the college. Colleges may know which high schools send students their way, but do not know what type of contact got students to the college door or what turned them away. Colleagues from baccalaureate institutions will know in detail where their students originated and their yield rates.

SEM theory as outlined in this book and elsewhere emphasizes the need for data. Like an overall SEM plan, an effective recruitment plan must be driven by data. How many inquiries do you receive each year? How many of those inquiring students complete an application? Of those applicants, how many take the placement test? And how many of those students who take the assessment meet with a counselor, enroll in classes, and actually attend class? It is important to determine these basic numbers in your funnel before developing a comprehensive recruitment plan. Unlike most universities, community college students do not start as prospects and end up enrolling. Community colleges have many more places for students to enter and exit the enrollment process. As a result, there are many more chances to lose students. Researching the points at which students are lost is very important.

There is one additional group that four-year institutions do not include in their funnel; that is, the students who show up on first day of the semester. These students have had no prior contact with the institution. They show-up out of nowhere, register, and begin attending classes. As open access institutions, this is unique to community colleges. This group must be researched to determine where they found out about the college and how the college, or something else, affected their decision to register for class.

An effective plan determines where within the funnel students are lost. Where is your funnel leaking? At one of the authors' prior institutions, we found that we were losing a large number of students after they completed the application for admissions and before they took the assessment. A large group of students also failed to enroll after they received their assessment results but before meeting with a counselor or advisor. By changing how the staff communicated with students about the enrollment process and the meaning of the assessment results, we dramatically reduced the number of students lost, thus increasing enrollment. While a very minor intervention, without the data from the funnel, we had no idea that barriers of our own creation were causing students to walk away from the institution.

Generating student enquiries stands at the top of the recruitment funnel. Traditionally, at community colleges, this has been done by sending staff to college fairs and individual district high schools, sending direct mail to high school seniors in our districts, or purchasing names of SAT or ACT takers. More recent efforts have relied on Web sites and e-mail. While traditional means of generating inquiries will continue, newer sources of technology popular with potential students require greater attention, including enhanced college Web sites and social networking sites, like Facebook, MySpace, and Twitter. In 2008, Neilson Online reported that 66.8 percent of internet users were using social networking to communicate, while only

65.1 percent also use email (Ostrow 2009). Facebook saw a 566 percent growth in 2008. These new technologies, and ones that we cannot even yet imagine, have the potential to be a gold mine of students if we learn how to use them effectively.

As you develop your SEM and recruitment plans, it is important to think about the goals you have for recruiting, an overall institutional marketing plan, and how you plan to communicate with prospective students, otherwise known as a communications plan.

● **RECRUITMENT GOALS**—increase enrollment; build the right mix of students; maintain current enrollment; bring in more international and out of district or out-of-state students; increase students in particular programs

● **MARKETING PLAN**—includes student recruitment, institutional branding (*see* Chapter 6, on page 81), and market placement (public awareness); need one plan for institution and one for individual departments

● **COMMUNICATION PLAN**—This is another important aspect of the recruitment process involving showcasing the distinctions and advantages of your institution to your primary audiences as part of a communication plan. To do so, you must develop a series of compelling messages and systematically distribute these to students throughout the enrollment process. The institution must create a strong "brand" image in the minds of prospective students, their families, and the communities served; this will strengthen the institution's overall image with the competitive recruitment market.

The Communication Plan

A wide-ranging communication plan should include a variety of different types of contacts with the prospective students. The types of contacts can include, but need not be limited to, direct mail publications, letters, emails, one-to-one contact, college fairs, phone calls, and social networking sites like Facebook or MySpace. Figures 8.2 and 8.3 offer graphical communication plans from community colleges.

Portland Community College's 2006 communication plan is a traditional mail plan run out of their student information systems' student recruitment module (*see* Figure 8.2). Each student inquiry is loaded into the SIS and generates mailings to the student over a six-week period. It is designed to stay in contact with prospective students. (Johnson 2006)

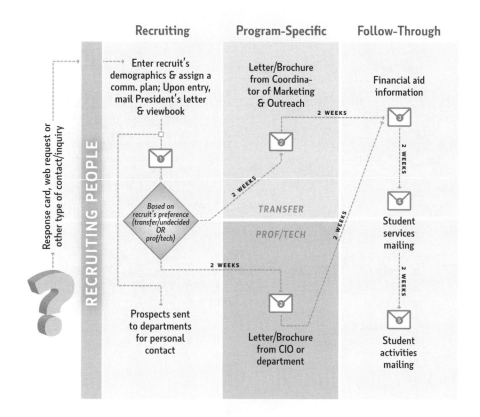

FIGURE 8.2

Example Traditional
Communication Plan

SOURCE: PORTLAND
COMMUNITY COLLEGE (2006)

An Ohio college has chosen to use electronic communication with their prospective students. Figure 8.3 (on page 138) shows how their approach differs from the mail plan that Portland Community College uses (Deutsch 2008).

RECRUITMENT PLAN REALITIES

In addition to the process and resultant recruitment plan, a number of other issues arise that should not come as a surprise. Here is a brief list of issues that the authors have seen emerge during the establishment of a recruitment plan.

FIGURE 8.3 ▶

Example Electronic
Communication Plan

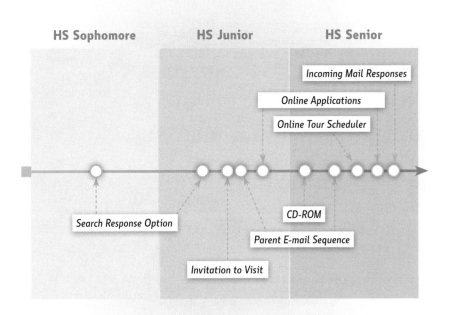

● **FLUIDITY:** A recruitment plan requires flexibility. Recruitment staff must be ready to react to campus and community issues with very short notice. At any given time, campus groups may identify the desire to recruit new groups of students to campus, *e.g.*, specific ethnic groups, low-income students, non-traditional students, or workers recently laid off at a nearby plant. Communication plan timelines will also need to shorten depending on the time of the year or situation that arises.

● **CONTINUOUS DEVELOPMENT OF OPPORTUNITIES:** Research will help locate opportunities to find new students. As talked about before, the key is determining where students drop out in the recruitment funnel and understanding where the students actually come from. Learning these and many more data will lead you to revelations about how the college can attract new students.

- **CONTINUOUS DEVELOPMENT OF RELATIONSHIPS:** Community relationships, inherent to the community college mission, are already robust in most cases. That said, as with any endeavor, room for improvement exists. Colleges that wish to improve their recruitment outcomes should actively engage in relationship building activities: become involved in the local chamber of commerce, Rotary, or visitor's bureau; schedule meetings with the local unemployment office, hospital human resources office, or mill or plant. Most local businesses and organizations want help with training or skill upgrades for their employees; perhaps they do not realize that your campus may be able to help them. Part of a good recruitment plan includes making people in your service area aware of your existence and desire to help.

- **INSTRUCTIONAL AREAS MAY DEVELOP PLANS UNIQUE TO THEIR MATCH MARKETING AND OUTREACH:** A great number of community colleges also have departments that do their own recruiting, especially those in the career technical areas. It is important to tie these plans into the overall institutional recruitment plan. You want to make sure that you are working together and not duplicating efforts and costs. If you can also tie your institutional communication plan into that of the specific program you can maximize the colleges contact with prospective students.

- **NEW ALLIES:** As you develop your new recruitment plan look for people on your campus who share your vision or programs and who need to improve their student enrollment. These allies will help carry the message of a new way of recruiting to other parts of the college. It is very important to find allies on the instruction side of the institution. Many times the faculty sees recruitment as meaning merely more headcount. Some areas of the college do not always understand that the benefits of marketing and outreach include communicating how the institution is meeting the needs of the service district. Recruitment (visibility) can be a great way to help with future bond measures, legislative issues, and public relations in general. Find allies in all parts of the institution that will carry recruitment and enrollment management to other areas of the college for which you may not have access.

- **DATA GENERATES A NEED FOR MORE DATA:** We can guarantee that once you start looking at your data, you will want more. Answering one research question will generate several more, and answering these questions with data will make your recruitment plan more effective. Do not rely on your institutional research office to gather data for you. One of the best things you can do is to learn to collect your own data.

● **PERSONNEL:** Throughout this chapter we have discussed ideas to enhance your recruitment of students. Please do not overlook the need for staff to respond to all the new inquires that your recruitment efforts will generate. We recently worked with a college that put in place a beautiful communications plan: they had new staff to hit the road recruiting students and a nice web and social network presence, but they were not responding to the inquiries. The community college had neglected to take into account the need for someone to mail out materials to prospective students, answer emails, or keep up on Facebook postings. While a great deal of money went into a sophisticated recruitment plan, stacks of college fair reply cards sat unanswered in the mail room. Why had their enrollment not increased? They had a recruitment plan. If colleges neglect inquiries into their programs, students will elect a more responsive institution to attend. Please do not forget about a plan for answering the prospective students request for information about your community college; it could be the most critical part of recruitment.

CONCLUSION

Community colleges, though well entrenched in our respective communities and open to all, will need to maintain an active role in recruiting students as our programs and communities change. As our institutions become more intentional in our efforts through planning and assessment, strategically recruiting to meet the intended goals of these efforts becomes crucial to managing enrollment while optimizing the use of limited resources.

It may be more important to recognize the growing importance of the recruitment function at community colleges and to begin to develop a plan where the environment is ready, rather than to try and engage the entire institution at once. Consider the history of recruitment at the institution and factors that influence how current structures have been designed and shaped by the culture. Collect and review data with those allies and develop some plans that support those who are willing to be early adopters. Engage a committed group in reviewing and researching models from the literature. Look at competitors and the practices of other institutions, even universities, to develop a plan and vision of recruitment. Assess and share successes that can create additional energy around the value of planning a recruitment strategy for other programs and the whole institution. The process for improving recruitment depends on the institution, its community, and its resources, but there is a growing awareness that recruitment is an important function that needs structure and direction in order to preserve the community college as a vital community educational resource.

SEM recruitment creates a foundation upon which to achieve sound resource planning. Student enrollment generates significant revenues for our institutions. Effective recruiting and recruitment planning contributes to resource maximization by targeting students for appropriate programs and matching demand and supply factors (facilities, instructors, support services), while supporting greater student success by improving the alignment of student goals and skills with program requirements. Becoming purposeful in recruitment supports the establishment of more predicable enrollments, which increases the effectiveness of other institutional planning efforts. As community colleges incorporate SEM into their planning and operations, the recruitment function will continue to evolve as a vital component for ensuring student and institutional success.

9

STRATEGIC ENROLLMENT MANAGEMENT'S
inancial Dynamics

by Kenneth Sharp

9   A common misconception is that budgets are static, only changing to cover wage increases or other mandated costs. In reality, budgets are dynamic things: they change as the institution changes. That is, they change as enrollments expand and contract and as economic conditions change. They are a reflection of an institution's priorities. Barr (2002) summed up the role of budgets stating, "the institutional budget reflects the plans, priorities, goals, and aspirations that drive the institution" (p. 30). Therefore, in the context of Strategic Enrollment Management (SEM), the budget really is a reflection of the institution's SEM Plan. In order to understand the financial dynamics of SEM, we must first develop a foundation by addressing some basic information about community colleges and higher education budgeting and finance.

WHY WORRY ABOUT SEM AND COMMUNITY COLLEGES?

Community colleges represent the largest segment of American higher education. In the fall of 2007, public two-year institutions enrolled over a third of the 18.2 million students in degree-granting colleges and universities (Knapp, Kelly-Reid, and Ginde 2009). Although community colleges impact the most students in the U.S. higher education system, community college issues are frequently overlooked in favor of four-year institutions. This probably results from four-year institutions having more staffing due to their size and researchers focusing on the institutions they are most familiar with (*i.e.*, their own four-year institutions).

In addition to serving the greatest proportion of the US higher education system, community colleges fulfill a wide-range of roles in the communities they serve.

Community colleges are frequently seen as leaders in workforce development with specialized programs and faculty perceived to have closer ties with industry than many of their four-year counterparts. As a result, many community colleges and community college pundits focus on jobs. Due to these perceptions, community colleges have been seen as a method for states to quickly and relevantly train dislocated workers. Additionally, the phenomenon of reverse transfer has become more prevalent. Reverse transfer refers to students attending four-year institutions or even graduates of four-year institutions transferring back to a community college to enroll in a program to develop job specific skills.

Community colleges also provide opportunities and access to those students either underprepared to attend a four-year institution or without access to a four-year institution for other reasons. Of new college freshmen at two-year institutions, 61 percent are not ready for college level work in mathematics, reading, and/or writing (Wirt, *et al.* 2004). Many four-year institutions require the resolution of these deficiencies before students are allowed to enroll. Many community colleges specialize in basic skills or remedial education, offering courses to help students prepare for a college curriculum. These institutions are also frequently viewed as a college of last resort or as an entry point to higher education for those students whose families have never attended college. In this capacity, they act as facilitators of social mobility providing environments supportive of those new to higher education.

Lastly, community colleges fulfill a role as transfer institutions. Community colleges provide an environment for students to complete lower division requirements prior to transferring to a four-year institution. Recently, the transfer role has been reexamined from a financial perspective. For example, a bill introduced in Virginia focused on providing incentives for students seeking four-year degrees to start out at community colleges (Keller 2007a). This incentive is due in part to community colleges being significantly less expensive per student full-time equivalent (FTE) than four-year institutions, particularly state flagship institutions, thus providing the state a savings for funding undergraduate enrollments at the community college rather than the four-year institution. The unstated assumption in this bill is that the quality of education received at a low-cost community college is the same as that provided at a four-year institution.

HIGHER EDUCATION FINANCES

Finances in higher education are very different from those of a traditional business. Theoretically, the purpose of a business is to generate profits through increased revenues and reduced costs. In higher education, administrators focus on educational excellence, prestige, and influence in an environment where institutions may not have the opportunities to lower costs through gains in productivity.

Two theories of higher educational costs are useful to keep in mind when examining both the cost and revenue structure of community colleges in developing a SEM plan. The first is that institutions of higher education belong to a class of organizations that do not have the ability to experience substantial gains in productivity, yet still must pay competitive wages for their highly educated workforce, thus resulting in increasing costs due to inflation (Baumol and Bowen 1966). Unlike businesses, the basic production process in higher education does not generally undergo substantive change. Also, institutions of higher education do not necessarily operate at the point of making the most efficient use of their productive capacity. Bowen (1980) developed the revenue theory of costs to describe this behavior. According to the revenue theory of costs:

- The dominant goals of institutions are educational excellence, prestige, and influence.
- In quest of excellence, prestige, and influence there is virtually no limit to the amount of money an institution could spend for seemingly fruitful educational ends.
- Each institution raises all the money possible.
- Each institution spends all it raises.
- The cumulative effect of the preceding four goals is toward ever-increasing expenditures.

Given this theoretical context, the next step is to examine the mechanics of higher education budgeting. Budgeting at most institutions can be seen as a three-step process. The first step is budget development, focusing on identifying the revenue sources available to the institution and making predictions regarding the actual amount of revenue the institution will receive. With a revenue projection in place the institution will go through a process of "divvying-up" the revenue to create expenditure budgets for the individual units of the institution. This "divvying-up" process is unique to each institution and its culture at any point in time. Strategies can range from allocating funds based on the direction provided by the president/chancellor to processes driven by an institution's shared governance structure. A successful SEM plan depends on activities identified in the SEM plan being funded per the SEM plan. Once the revenue and expenditure estimates are finally agreed upon, the budget is set.

The second step in the budget process is budget management. At many institutions, budget management means that employees seek to spend no more than the amount budgeted in the areas reported to management. Given the power of modern enterprise resource planning (ERP) systems, many institutions view budgets dynamically where revenues, in particular those generated by student enrollments, are matched up with expenditures. At these institutions, with enrollments projected to decline or grow, budgets are adjusted accordingly.

The final step in the budgeting process is the analysis of budgets, revenues, and expenditures—the review phase. This process allows management to identify where revenues were generated, where expenditures occurred, and any variances with the budget. Budget variances inform management as to the quality of the budget projections made throughout the year and the ability of college faculty, staff, and administrators to act as stewards of their respective funds.

A SEM PERSPECTIVE ON BUDGETING

From a financial perspective, developing and managing a SEM plan appears similar to developing and managing any strategic plan. In the planning process, two ways to view budgets exist: as either a constraint or an enabler to the plan depending on your institution's paradigm. Either way, budgets represent plans for the utilization of resources, their flexibility depending on a college's specific environment.

Before beginning a SEM plan, laying the financial groundwork for the SEM planning process involves a significant amount of work. The institution's financial information must be analyzed in the same way an institution's enrollment patterns must be analyzed to develop the starting point for SEM planning. Given that SEM planning constitutes a cross-functional activity, financial information will often need translation into a form easily understood by decision makers who are not finance experts. Bontrager and Brown (2008) offer a model for integrating SEM and budget planning described later in this chapter.

SOURCES OF REVENUES

Community colleges potentially have several revenue streams behaving very differently from each other that can influence SEM planning decisions. For the sake of simplicity, the focus in this chapter will be on that commonly referred to as general fund operations. This includes most core instructional and related support activities. Contract and grant related instruction will not be specifically addressed as these activities should be self-contained. Although there are many nuances state-by-state, primarily the three sources for community college general fund operations include, tuition and fees, state appropriations, and, in some cases, local taxes. The behaviors of each of these funding sources will have a significant impact on SEM planning.

Tuition and Fees

Tuition and fees represent what most students generally see as the cost of attending college. Interestingly, higher education is one of the few sections of the economy where consumers (students) generally pay a price less than the cost of the product or service. Tuition and fees are usually related to the amount of instruction received by the student, but not always directly. Tuition, in the simplest case, can be charged by the credit hour, where each additional credit hour generates a consistent additional dollar value of tuition. Tuition can also be based on plateaus and assessed at a flat rate per credit hour, up to a certain amount, generally between nine and twelve credit hours; at this point tuition is either constant or constant up to a specified credit hour limit, where tuition continues to increase at the standard per-credit-hour rate. Another common methodology involves charging a flat rate for tuition regardless of the number of credit hours taken. While just a sampling of the tuition schemes used among community colleges, each of these cases presents unique challenges for SEM revenue planning.

In the case of tuition being charged at a flat per-credit-hour rate, each additional student enrollment results in additional revenues for the credit hours taken. As enrollments and student FTEs increase, so do tuition revenues as shown in Figure 9.1(A); conversely, as student FTEs decrease tuition revenues follow.

FIGURE 9.1 ▶

Three Tuition Models

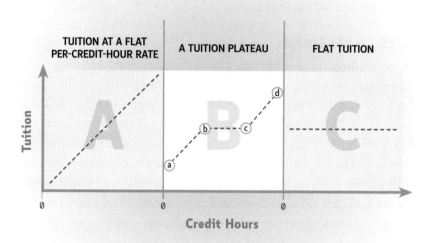

In the case of a tuition plateau, each additional credit hour a student takes may or may not result in additional revenues, depending on the location of each individual student on the tuition rate curve illustrated in Figure 9.1(B). At point a, each additional credit hour of enrollment will generate additional tuition up to point b. Enrollments from points b to c yield no additional revenues, and enrollments to the right of point d generate additional revenues. When planning for revenues with a tuition plateau, the institution must monitor their efforts in generating additional enrollment to ensure they are properly accounting for the plateau.

For institutions with a flat tuition rate, as shown in Figure 9.1(C), accounting for revenues generated by additional students is greatly simplified: new students generate additional revenues, and existing students who enroll in additional credit hours generate no additional revenues.

Non-resident tuition is frequently used as a vehicle for community colleges to collect the full cost of non-resident student enrollments that in many cases may not be subsidized by state funding formulas. Many four-year institutions and some two-year institutions specifically recruit non-resident students because the additional revenues they generate can be used to help offset or subsidize the costs for resident students. A non-resident student often pays in-state or district tuition rates for the first six to nine credit hours of enrollment. In this particular case, revenues should be treated much in the same manner as resident students.

Student fees must also be considered as part of the revenue calculus. Student fees generally come in three varieties: term based, course based, and credit hour based. Term based fees, charged once per enrolled term, include campus computing fees, matriculation fees, and registration fees. Revenues generated by these fees can be readily calculated from the institution's student headcount.

State Appropriations

State budgets are cyclical in nature. During periods of financial exigency, budgets are cut, reducing or eliminating discretionary programs in an effort to balance budgets. During periods of increasing revenues, states respond to the pent up demand for cut programs by reinstating budgets. Further, as revenues increase, lawmakers are pressured to spend down surpluses and respond to calls for reduced taxes by their constituencies. The financial demands of Medicaid increase the complexity of the state budget equation. A joint report by the National Governors Association and the National Association of State Budget Officers (2006) referred to Medicaid as a major budget issue for states. Medicaid currently makes up 22.9 percent of state budgets with an estimated 8 percent annual growth rate over the next decade.

On the revenue side, structural changes in the economy also impact state budgets. Consumer spending patterns are changing: consumers spend a greater portion of their incomes on services than in the past, and sales taxes are not generally collected on services. A second major change to state revenues is a result of the Internet. With limited exceptions, states cannot collect sales taxes on Internet related transactions.

Local Taxes

Local taxes comprise a third category of revenues available to some community colleges. In most cases, local taxes for community colleges are similar to the taxes collected by K–12 districts. Generally two variables drive local taxes: the assessment rate and the assessed value of the property. The assessment rate is generally driven by statute, thus it is generally fixed or rarely fluctuates. The assessed value of the property can change on a regular basis (unless frozen by state or local statute). As property values increase, tax revenues increase. As property values decrease, with declines in the economy, so do tax revenues. The latter can be especially challenging in times of economic decline, such as those we presently face, when demand for community college services typically increase. Although local taxes are not driven by enrollments, they must be accounted for where appropriate when developing a SEM plan.

Of these three potential revenue streams for community colleges, college management only has control over tuition and fees and can exert limited influence on state appropriations and local taxes. This being the case, colleges must remain cognizant of changes in state appropriations and local taxes while making SEM decisions.

COST CONCEPTS

Just as SEM decision makers must understand the nuances associated with their revenue streams, they must also understand the nuances of their cost structures. Key frequently overlooked cost concepts for community colleges include the differences between marginal and average costs, the implications of facility costs, and the implications for increasing demand on the institution.

Marginal Costs vs. Average Costs

When creating, managing, and evaluating a SEM plan a key metric is the change in cost per change in student enrollment. It is tempting to examine the average-cost-per-student as evaluation criteria and make projections using this metric. Unfortunately, the average-cost-per-student does not provide the costs for changes in student enrollments. A more useful metric is the marginal-cost-per-student, which by definition provides the change in cost per change in student enrollment. As an illustration, let us assume a small department with the majority of the classes being taught by full-time faculty and a small number of classes being taught by part-time faculty. Assume, as is the case at most institutions, that full-time faculty receive significantly greater compensation than the full-time-equivalent part-time faculty. In this case, the average-cost-per-student is based on most of the classes being taught by full-time faculty. On the other hand, what is the cost of adding additional students? Chances are that part-time faculty will be added as opposed to full-time faculty, making the marginal-cost-per-student significantly lower than the average-cost-per-student.

Facilities Costs

One of the constraints on SEM plans easily overlooked is the physical infrastructure of the institution. Not all spaces are equally suited to all instructional activities. Many institutions have created specialized instructional spaces of limited value to programs other than the program for which they were designed. At many institutions, programs "own" classrooms. This kind of ownership can lead to underutilization of the facility and, if prevented, can provide valuable needed space on campus for other programs or a combination of other programs. Another facility constraint frequently encountered is "10–2 syndrome." The term "10–2 syndrome" refers to the predisposition to schedule all classes between the hours of 10 am and 2 pm and indicates that the institution is operating at capacity because no room exists for additional enrollments between the hours of 10 am and 2 pm. Behind personnel, facilities frequently comprise the second largest category of expense at community colleges, and their effective and efficient utilization should be addressed when appropriate in the SEM planning process.

Demand/Enrollment

Notwithstanding the current difficult financial environment, an increase in the demand for higher education is projected. Undergraduate enrollment is expected to increase from 14.8 million undergraduate students in 2004 to 16.9 million undergraduates in 2015 (Wirt, *et al.* 2004) nationwide. Data from *The Chronicle of Higher Education* (2005) indicates growth among two-year institutions from 6.3 million in 2004 to 7.1 million in 2014, an increase of 13 percent over ten years. Some high growth states display even more significant increases in demand. For example, the California Postsecondary Commission (2005) estimates that between 2003 and 2013 the demand for higher education at the community college level will increase by nearly 29 percent, and the Arizona Board of Regents (2004) projects a 34 percent increase in the demand for higher education from 2005 through 2015. The trend of decreased funding combined with increased enrollment is not new. According to Vaughan (2005), since the 1960s community colleges have been increasing enrollments in the name of open admissions while state funding did not keep up or was even cut.

IDENTIFYING SEM INVESTMENTS AND MEASURABLE OUTCOMES

In designing the SEM financial plan, institutions frequently do a good job of identifying costs, but not identifying the returns to financial decisions. As an example, if an institution examines the effect of increasing tutoring as part of a SEM financial plan, the costs of a tutor, including space, support staff, furniture, and the other related costs can be readily calculated. However, institutions generally experience less success with identifying the impact on enrollments. How is the impact identified? Do new students attend the institution because of the increased tutoring? Are students more successful? There are essentially four methods to project the enrollment response: experimentation, literature searches, peer institution experiences, and the experiences and expertise resident within the institution.

Literature, particularly the peer-reviewed literature is rich with examples of responses to changes in institutional characteristics. Unfortunately, much of the literature concentrates on four-year institutions, where the findings may be substantially different from those at two-year institutions. Even among two-year public community colleges, Sharp (2007) found significant differences in the response to changes in enrollments among the different Carnegie classifications of two-year institutions.

Peer institutions can also serve as a source of information. Peer institutions frequently make changes or experiment with programs of interest to other institutions; information on these programs can usually be found at national and regional conferences. In the author's experience, the findings presented are often subject to positive biases with institutions selectively interpreting results. Further, peer results are subject to the same warnings as results from experiments performed at your own institution—namely, the level of rigor applied to the natural experiment and the analytical rigor applied.

Experience and expert knowledge is probably the quickest and easiest method of evaluation. Collectively the faculty, staff, and administration at each institution potentially has hundreds of years of experience in the community college environment, including observations regarding how changes in institutional characteristics impact student enrollments. These observations have value; however, they frequently have not included a systematic analysis of the impact on student enrollments. This method should be used if no other sources of information are available.

IMPLEMENTING THE SEM PLANNING MODEL

The development and implementation of SEM plans have been addressed by several authors and are addressed elsewhere in the book for the particular environment of the community college. Bontrager and Brown (2008) have further delineated a framework that integrates the role of finance in the SEM planning process. This framework consists of four phases: developing comprehensive enrollment goals; identifying strategic enrollment investments and measurable outcomes; tracking enrollment, net revenue and budget outcomes; and creating reinvestment strategies.

Phase 1: Developing Comprehensive Enrollment Goals

The first phase of an institution's SEM plan is developing comprehensive enrollment goals. This process is not as quick and simple as it may seem at first glance. To develop comprehensive enrollment goals, an institution must go through a process similar to a strategic planning process to formulate a vision of what the institution could or should be. Once this is determined, the institution can develop its actual enrollment goals required to meet the institutional vision. Enrollment goals generally are not represented by one enrollment number, but by a bundle of student and institutional characteristics, including:

- Increasing student access
- Increasing enrollment in programs with socially desirable student characteristics
- Targeting specific student demographics
- Increasing community participation rates
- Increasing out of district/out of state/out of country enrollments
- Increasing retention
- Increasing student goal attainment (student goals may or may not include graduation)
- Development of unique programs/centers

As alluded to earlier, the process of developing enrollment goals is long and involved. The process should include stakeholders from across the institution as well as members of the local community serviced by the college, particularly given that community colleges have been characterized as local institutions (Cohen and Brawer 1996).

Phase 2: Identifying Strategic Enrollment Investments and Measurable Outcomes

Once the institution has established enrollment goals, the next phase is to develop the plans for achieving those goals, identifying both costs and the measurable enrollment results each plan is anticipated to generate. While going through the plan development process, often plans beget additional plans as the full implications of the enrollment goals are fully understood.

Each plan developed to achieve an institutional enrollment goal can be seen as a strategic enrollment investment. By focusing on plans as strategic enrollment investments, institutions must ask themselves the same questions a business might in a similar situation. Namely, what does it cost? What are the potential returns from the investment? How can each investment be evaluated against other alternatives?

Identifying the costs associated with a strategic enrollment investment should be a relatively easy task from an accounting perspective. From a political perspective, it is not always as easy. The costs associated with proposals may be understated to provide additional support for a strategic enrollment investment, making the investment look more desirable than reality. Conversely, strategic enrollment investment costs may be overstated if there is a clear case for the investment, and a proposer has additional items they would like to have funded. Neither of these scenarios is healthy for developing an effective SEM plan. Participants need to be completely honest about the full costs of a strategic enrollment investment decision.

Just as participants in the SEM planning process need to be objective about the costs of a program, they also need to be as accurate and objective as possible when estimating the enrollments generated by a strategic enrollment investment. As was the case with costs, there may be pressures on participants to overstate or understate the enrollments resulting from strategic enrollment investment decisions. Unfortunately, no "one size fits all" answer as to where an institution should make exists. Each institution is unique as is each institution's student population and environment. The important parameter in deciding which initiative to invest in is the dollar return for each expected outcome. Developing a list of potential investment initiatives involves a brainstorming effort, with evaluation following the establishment of a complete list. When an institution has multiple initiatives from which to choose, return on investment (ROI) serves as an evaluation tool. ROI is calculated by identifying the additional revenue generated by an initiative and dividing by the cost of implementing the initiative. For any investment decision, the ROI should be greater than 1.0, which represents the break-even point. Higher ROIs are better investment decisions than lower ROIs. ROI does not measure the utility provided to students or to the community; it is only an indicator of financial value.

Phase 3: Tracking Enrollment, Net Revenue, and Budget Outcomes

After taking the time to develop enrollment goals and make strategic enrollment investments based on the enrollment related outcomes, your institution should evaluate its results. Monitor strategic investments decisions to ensure the costs incurred are consistent with the budget. Further, analyze changes in enrollment to ensure any changes attributed to strategic enrollment investments specifically resulted from the investment as opposed to other influences.

Phase 4: Creating Reinvestment Strategies

Generating enrollment growth takes time, energy, and resources from the individual departments within institutions. For example, academic units must hire additional faculty, instructional staff, and supplies; student development units must provide for additional student contacts; and administrative units must provide additional support to staff and faculty as well as increased physical and IT infrastructure for students. To provide this additional support, these units will need to receive resources to fund enrollment growth. SEM financial planning allows institutions to identify the units contributing to the growth, how much they contribute to growth, and provides a mechanism for funding those units based on the enrollments generated.

Several community colleges have used similar funding mechanisms referred to as enrollment-based budgeting. The usual implementation of enrollment-based budgeting focuses on identifying the marginal costs and revenues generated by a program and adjusting the program budget as enrollments change. The key difference between the funding mechanisms used in enrollment-based budgeting and those used in the financial component of a SEM plan is that enrollment-based budgeting is reactive whereas SEM is proactive. In other words, the SEM plan adjusts budgets based on the planned enrollments, whereas most enrollment-based budgets undergo adjustment after enrollments have changed. Despite the differences, several of the lessons learned implementing enrollment-based budgeting also apply when implementing a SEM financial plan. As an example, enrollment-based budgeting has been implemented at several organizational levels including at individual college campuses, at the college level, and at the college district level. This proves by extension that SEM financial plans can also be implemented at the campus, college, or college district level.

One of the most powerful concepts in using this funding mechanism is the way it incentivizes growth by providing resources to those growing programs most in need. Incentivizing growth, however, may have unintended consequences that SEM practitioners need to be prepared to address. In the early stages of implementation, it is possible that faculty will view incentivizing growth as a form of "industrialization" where their departments are essentially being paid for piecework. Another image created is that of the institution becoming an "FTE factory" where the objective is to maximize the production of student enrollments. Prevent these paradigms by avoiding the use of business and/or industrial jargon and focusing on the benefits created to the students and the community as a result of the additional enrollments.

Another interesting cultural barrier to be aware of is the structure of the incentive program. Generally, one of three methodologies is used: basing the incentives on average costs, marginal costs, or a flat rate. Business office staff tends to favor incentives using average or marginal costs as they tie revenues to expenses. As a result, a program with class size restrictions, high proportions of full-time faculty, and extensive supplies and services requirements would receive a much larger incentive per student FTE than a program with no class size restriction, lower proportions of full-time faculty, and requiring few supplies or services. In this case, I have been approached by faculty members representing low incentive (low marginal cost) disciplines who posited that the institution did not value the students in their disciplines as much as students in higher incentive (higher marginal cost) disciplines. This paradigm is much more difficult to resolve than the "FTE factory" paradigm because of the assignment of "value" to a discipline and a discipline's students; it must be addressed with care.

SEM FINANCIAL PLANNING IN ACTION

Now that the particulars of establishing and managing the financial portion of the SEM plan have been discussed, a detailed example follows.

Phase 1: Developing Comprehensive Enrollment Goals

Hypothetical Community College (HCC) has decided to embark on developing a SEM plan. To keep things simple, the administration has agreed to focus on a project they have identified as "Improving Student Outcomes." The primary objective of the "Improving Student Outcomes" project is to increase retention and graduation rates and to do it within the resources provided by the tuition and fees generated as a result of student retention.

Before quantifying the institution's objectives, the institution should collect and examine their existing financial and enrollment data. The financial and enrollment data for HCC is listed in Table 9.1 (on page 160). At a minimum, the enrollment, costs, average cost per student FTE, marginal cost per FTE, and net revenues per student FTE for each academic department at HCC should be identified. In addition, at the institutional level, enrollment costs and marginal costs should be identified. Most institutions have readily available institutional level data as the information is required for financial statements and for submission by all Title IV recipients to the National Center for Education Statistics (NCES) for entry into the Integrated Postsecondary Education Data System (IPEDS).

With the institution's base data collected, HCC should next develop a multi-year base budget model, used to examine the financial and enrollment effects of a SEM initiative before any changes are introduced such as inflation or natural enrollment growth. Table 9.2 (on page 161) contains the multi-year base budget model for Hypothetical Community College. Multi-year budget models can be created in whatever length is appropriate for the institution and the institution's SEM initiatives.

Once HCC collects their financial and enrollment information, they are in a position to quantify their objectives. The retention goal becomes to increase year one to year two retention rates to 80 percent as measured by the number of students moving from the completion of thirty credit hours to the completion of forty-five credit hours within three years. The decision to use the number of thirty to forty-five credit hour completers is made because a significant number of HCC's students attend part-time and may not necessarily be classifiable in cohorts. The graduation goal becomes to increase the number of graduates by 10 percent within two years. Note that both goals under the umbrella of "Improving Student Outcomes" are clearly defined, quantifiable, reasonably achievable, and have an expected period of performance identified.

Phase 2: Identifying Strategic Enrollment Investments and Measurable Outcomes

Phase two of developing the SEM financial plan comprises identifying strategic enrollment investments and the measurable outcomes from those investments. In

TABLE 9.1. HYPOTHETICAL COMMUNITY COLLEGE BASELINE ENROLLMENT AND FINANCIAL DATA

	Annual Enrollment¹	Last Year's Expenditures	Cost per Student¹			Revenue per Student¹		State Appropriations per Student¹	Tuition & Fee Revenues	Other Revenues
			Average	Marginal	Loaded	Marginal	Net			
DEPARTMENT										
Allied Health	85	811,769	9,550	7,758	8,694	6,099	(2,595)		518,394	
Automotive	71	423,667	5,967	3,716	4,652	4,147	(505)		294,446	
Business	368	1,142,037	3,103	2,246	3,182	4,147	965		1,526,140	
English	138	333,441	2,416	3,001	3,937	4,147	210		572,303	
IT²	202	1,092,875	5,410	3,588	4,524	4,147	(377)		837,718	
Languages	188	507,047	2,697	2,298	3,234	4,147	913		779,659	
Liberal Arts	196	472,011	2,408	1,712	2,648	4,147	1,499		812,836	
Manufacturing	146	1,136,805	7,786	5,895	6,831	4,147	(2,684)		605,480	
Mathematics	380	1,066,503	2,807	1,942	2,878	4,147	1,269		1,575,906	
Social Sciences	155	362,959	2,342	1,875	2,811	4,147	1,336		642,804	
Subtotal	*1,929*	*7,349,115*	*3,810*	*2,875*	*3,811*	*4,233*	*422*		*8,165,683*	
Other Instructional Programs		816,568		178						
Student Development		2,449,705		758						
Finance & Administration		1,306,509								
Fixed Costs		3,429,587								
College Administration		979,882								
Total	*1,929*	*16,331,366*	*8,466*	*3,811*				*4,912,647*	*8,165,683*	*3,266,273*

¹ FTE (Full-Time Equivalent)
² Information Technology

the case of HCC, one of the base assumptions is funding the strategy through the generation of new revenues. The revenues and costs associated with HCC's strategy to "Improve Student Outcomes" are illustrated in Table 9.3 (on page 162). HCC identifies two action items associated with their strategy: to increase advising and provide enhanced tutoring. Increasing advising in this case refers to hiring an additional academic advisor to ensure the proper advisement of students for their academic programs and to work as a facilitator for students in navigating the college

TABLE 9.2. FIVE-YEAR BASE BUDGET MODEL

	Base Year	Year 1	Year 2	Year 3	Year 4	Year 5
REVENUES						
State Appropriations	4,912,647	4,912,647	4,912,647	4,912,647	4,912,647	4,912,647
Tuition and Fees	8,165,683	8,165,683	8,165,683	8,165,683	8,165,683	8,165,683
Other Revenues	3,266,273	3,266,273	3,266,273	3,266,273	3,266,273	3,266,273
Total Revenues	*16,344,603*	*16,344,603*	*16,344,603*	*16,344,603*	*16,344,603*	*16,344,603*
DEPARTMENT						
Allied Health	811,769	811,769	811,769	811,769	811,769	811,769
Automotive	423,667	423,667	423,667	423,667	423,667	423,667
Business	1,142,037	1,142,037	1,142,037	1,142,037	1,142,037	1,142,037
English	333,441	333,441	333,441	333,441	333,441	333,441
Information Technology	1,092,875	1,092,875	1,092,875	1,092,875	1,092,875	1,092,875
Languages	507,047	507,047	507,047	507,047	507,047	507,047
Liberal Arts	472,011	472,011	472,011	472,011	472,011	472,011
Manufacturing	1,136,805	1,136,805	1,136,805	1,136,805	1,136,805	1,136,805
Mathematics	1,066,503	1,066,503	1,066,503	1,066,503	1,066,503	1,066,503
Social Sciences	362,959	362,959	362,959	362,959	362,959	362,959
Subtotal	*7,349,115*	*7,349,115*	*7,349,115*	*7,349,115*	*7,349,115*	*7,349,115*
Other Instructional Programs	816,568	816,568	816,568	816,568	816,568	816,568
Student Development	2,449,705	2,449,705	2,449,705	2,449,705	2,449,705	2,449,705
Finance & Administration	1,306,509	1,306,509	1,306,509	1,306,509	1,306,509	1,306,509
Fixed Costs	3,429,587	3,429,587	3,429,587	3,429,587	3,429,587	3,429,587
College Administration	979,882	979,882	979,882	979,882	979,882	979,882
Total	*16,331,366*	*16,331,366*	*16,331,366*	*16,331,366*	*16,331,366*	*16,331,366*
Net of Operations	13,237	13,237	13,237	13,237	13,237	13,237
Cumulative Net	13,237	26,475	39,712	52,949	66,187	79,424
Annual Enrollment (FTE)	1,929	1,929	1,929	1,929	1,929	1,929
Cost per FTE	8,466	8,466	8,466	8,466	8,466	8,466
State Appropriations per FTE	2,547	2,547	2,547	2,547	2,547	2,547
Tuition & Fees per FTE	4,233	4,233	4,233	4,233	4,233	4,233

system. Enhanced tutoring is selected in response to low completion rates in basic skills courses, mathematics in particular. Additional mathematics tutoring resources will be made available to students to help guarantee their proficiency with the math skills required to facilitate success in their academic programs. Note that in this example, if HCC only examines the first year of the program, the results would be a loss of $13,109 that, if further years are not examined, would result in rejecting the

TABLE 9.3. REVENUES AND COSTS ASSOCIATED WITH THE STRATEGY TO "IMPROVE STUDENT OUTCOMES"

	Base Year	Year 1	Year 2	Year 3	Year 4	Year 5
Enrollment by Credits Earned						
15	722	722	722	722	722	722
30	506	506	506	506	506	506
45	389	389	389	389	389	389
60	312	312	312	312	312	312
Total Enrollments	1,929	1,929	1,929	1,929	1,929	1,929
Year 1–Year 2 Retention (%)	76.9	76.9	76.9	76.9	76.9	76.9
Graduates	358	358	358	358	358	358
IMPROVE STUDENT OUTCOMES						
SEM Costs						
Increase Advising		35,000	35,000	35,000	35,000	35,000
Enhanced Tutoring		10,000	10,000	10,000	10,000	10,000
Total SEM Costs		45,000	45,000	45,000	45,000	45,000
Enrollment by Credits Earned						
15	722	722	722	722	722	722
30	506	526	541	552	552	552
45	389	416	432	443	451	451
60	312	340	359	368	371	371
Total Enrollments	1,929	2,005	2,054	2,085	2,096	2,096
Graduates	358	390	412	422	426	426
Increase in Graduates (%)	0	9.0	15.0	18.0	19.0	19.0
Change in Enrollment [1]	0	76	125	156	167	167
Net Revenue per FTE	422	422	422	422	422	422
Net Revenue [2]		31,891	52,769	65,918	70,519	70,519
Net for Initiative		(13,109)	7,769	20,918	25,519	25,519

[1] Attributable to SEM
[2] Generated from tuition

initiative. By year three, the initiatives are planned to have paid for themselves and actually generate revenues above and beyond the cost of the project.

Phase 3: Tracking Enrollment, Net Revenue and Budget Outcomes

Once an institution has developed a SEM plan, monitoring the implementation of the plan is key. The revenues, expenditures, and enrollments should be monitored closely to ensure the success of the plan and changes evaluated to identify those associated with the SEM plan. If changes in revenues, expenditures, or enrollments are associated with the SEM plan, the institution should evaluate the impact of the changes on the plan to see if the action items should be updated or changed. In any case, conduct the SEM planning process at least on a yearly basis to ensure the institution is meeting its overall objectives and to adjust the plan to identify new opportunities.

Phase 4: Creating Reinvestment Strategies

Once the initiatives are evaluated, they are allocated into the planning budget. This allows for a holistic view of the revenues and expenditures. Additionally, this provides a basis for evaluating the actual results of the SEM planning initiatives as well as a foundation for developing the full institutional budget with escalation for inflation and changes revenue rates.

The allocated results for HCC's "Improve Student Outcomes" SEM strategy are presented in Table 9.4 (on page 164). Note the increases in tuition and fees revenues resulting from the increased enrollments. Departmental expenditures also increase as each department must pay the marginal costs associated with educating the students who no longer drop out of the academic programs at the same rate. Similarly, both other instructional services and student development experience increases associated with increased student retention. The direct costs for the enhanced tutoring and increased advising action items have also been included in the other instructional services and student development budgets respectively.

CONCLUSION

Community college practitioners are in a complex, dynamic environment. They attempt to respond to the needs of their communities, their students, and other

TABLE 9.4. ALLOCATED RESULTS FROM THE "IMPROVE STUDENT OUTCOMES" SEM STRATEGY

	Base Year	Year 1	Year 2	Year 3	Year 4	Year 5
Revenues						
State Appropriations	4,912,647	4,912,647	4,912,647	4,912,647	4,912,647	4,912,647
Tuition and Fees	8,165,683	8,485,495	8,694,865	8,826,726	8,872,867	8,872,867
Other Revenues	3,266,273	3,266,273	3,266,273	3,266,273	3,266,273	3,266,273
Total Revenues	*16,344,603*	*16,664,415*	*16,873,785*	*17,005,646*	*17,051,787*	*17,051,787*
Department						
Allied Health	811,769	837,598	854,506	865,155	868,881	868,881
Automotive	423,667	434,002	440,767	445,027	446,518	446,518
Business	1,142,037	1,174,410	1,195,602	1,208,949	1,213,622	1,213,621
English	333,441	349,661	360,282	366,969	369,309	369,309
Information Technology	1,092,875	1,121,261	1,139,847	1,151,550	1,155,646	1,155,648
Languages	507,047	523,967	535,046	542,024	544,464	544,464
Liberal Arts	472,011	485,153	493,759	499,177	501,074	501,074
Manufacturing	1,136,805	1,170,514	1,192,583	1,206,484	1,211,347	1,211,347
Mathematics	1,066,503	1,095,405	1,114,329	1,126,248	1,130,419	1,130,418
Social Sciences	362,959	374,344	381,796	386,489	388,131	388,131
Subtotal	*7,349,115*	*7,566,316*	*7,708,517*	*7,798,073*	*7,829,410*	*7,829,410*
Other Instructional Programs	816,568	840,018	848,822	854,367	856,307	856,307
Student Development	2,449,705	2,541,975	2,579,462	2,603,074	2,611,336	2,611,336
Finance & Administration	1,306,509	1,306,509	1,306,509	1,306,509	1,306,509	1,306,509
Fixed Costs	3,429,587	3,429,587	3,429,587	3,429,587	3,429,587	3,429,587
College Administration	979,882	979,882	979,882	979,882	979,882	979,882
Total	*16,331,366*	*16,664,286*	*16,852,779*	*16,971,491*	*17,013,031*	*17,013,031*
Net of Operations	13,237	128	21,006	34,155	38,756	38,756
Cumulative Net	13,237	13,366	34,372	68,527	107,283	146,040
Annual Enrollment (FTE)	1,929	2,006	2,086	2,170	2,257	2,347
Cost per FTE	8,466	8,307	8,077	7,821	7,539	7,249
State Appropriations per FTE	2,547	2,449	2,355	2,264	2,177	2,093
Tuition & Fees per FTE	4,233	4,230	4,167	4,068	3,932	3,781
Enrollment Projections (FTE)						
Allied Health	85	88	91	92	92	92
Automotive	71	74	76	77	77	77
Business	368	382	392	398	400	400
English	138	143	147	149	150	150
Information Technology	202	210	215	218	219	219
Languages	188	195	200	203	204	204
Liberal Arts	196	204	209	212	213	213
Manufacturing	146	152	155	158	159	159
Mathematics	380	395	405	411	413	413
Social Sciences	155	161	165	168	168	168
Total	*1,929*	*2,005*	*2,054*	*2,085*	*2,096*	*2,096*

stakeholders in order to provide cost effective, quality services. SEM is a planning tool that can be used to help these practitioners meet the needs of their stakeholders. The financial component of SEM is an enabler of the overall SEM plan.

STRATEGIC ENROLLMENT MANAGEMENT AND
Campus Leadership

by Christine Kerlin *and* William Serrata

10

The phrases "strategic enrollment management" and "campus leadership" are inextricably intertwined—deeply dependent on the buy-in of campus leaders and particularly on the support of, and championing by, the president.

Successful SEM planning derives from the involvement of the executive leaders of the campus. Their involvement can be exemplified by integrating SEM with the college's overall strategic plan, by aligning SEM plans with the budget process, by supporting SEM implementation through recognition that it is an institution-wide responsibility, and by continuous communication through the assessment and revitalization processes.

These are indeed lofty ideals, and the prospect of achieving this Nirvana can be daunting to those contemplating the SEM process on their campus or in their system, as well as to those who are in the middle of SEM.

In this chapter we will attempt to make the case for leadership buy-in, describe some of the leadership ingredients that make SEM work—and work well—and how to build a leadership approach to SEM.

THE CASE FOR LEADERSHIP

The case for strong leadership in SEM has its roots in describing SEM with particular relevance to community and technical colleges:

Enrollment management is a comprehensive and coordinated process that enables a college to identify enrollment goals that are allied with its multiple missions, its strategic plan, its environment, and its resources, and to reach those goals through the effective integration of administrative processes, student services, curriculum planning, and market analysis (Kerlin 2008, p. 11).

This definition acknowledges first of all the multiple missions of the community and technical colleges (CTCs) that make enrollment management such a challenge. Secondly, it outlines the multiple areas that should be integrated into the planning. The ability of a college or system to meet these challenges requires high-level buy-in and involvement.

During the Strategic Enrollment Management VIII Conference, Dolence (1998) described Strategic Enrollment Management Condition Alert Status Level 4: Strategic Enrollment Management in the following fashion:

- SEM aligns with the campus environment
- SEM integrates decision making
- SEM fused with academics
- SEM philosophy: reviewing every college policy and determining its effect on enrollment
- SEM embedded: a "culture" of enrollment management permeates day to day operations

In order to reach the highest SEM level described by Dolence, strong campus leadership and the infusion of SEM principles within the campus leadership are prerequisites.

Similarly, Bontrager (2004a) describes the optimal structure for campus enrollment management as follows:

Finally, there is the enrollment management division, in which the key offices and functions related to enrollment management are brought together under the leadership of a senior-level administrator. This model reflects the highest degree of institutional commitment to influencing enrollments. Additionally, it increases the likelihood that enrollment management efforts will be led by an enrollment specialist, i.e., an individual with experience and training specific to managing college and university enrollments (p. 14).

Finally, Whiteside described the concept of SEM stating, "SEM is more about exercising influence than it is about exercising control" (1998, slide 8).

Dolence, Bontrager, and Whiteside, along with Kerlin's definition, all point to the importance of campus leadership in SEM.

The reasons for engaging in SEM strategies are many. For most institutions, though, the adoption of an enrollment management approach effectively meets the challenges of expected or unexpected peaks and valleys in enrollment that seem somewhat endemic to an open door institution pledged to serve its community. It is a way to develop honest budget and facilities plans based on an informed vision of enrollment patterns and the income and expenditures linked to those patterns. It is a way to bring the college together around instructional planning and student success and outcomes goals, especially those subject to increasing external scrutiny.

SEM can strike fear and trembling into some members of the college community. It can be seen as a calculated approach that undermines free access and the integrity of the mission of the institution. Staff of certain programs and services might be afraid of marginalization as other types of enrollment initiatives are emphasized. It can be seen as an add-on by those who already feel overloaded and under-resourced.

Hossler and Kalsbeek (2008) acknowledge some of the reasons why an institution might back away from SEM, but posit the following question: "Should colleges and universities just let their enrollments happen?" They suggest that:

...few presidents or boards of trustees would be willing to take a laissez-faire attitude with student enrollment, to be nonchalant about the dominant source of institutional revenue, to be undisciplined and unintentional and uninformed in the functions and processes that have such a powerful impact on the health, mission and vitality of the institution (p. 4).

The case for SEM, then, lies in a web of pressures.
- Assuring that our missions for access and service are met
- Managing our resources in the face of high and low enrollment trends

- Aligning our programs and services with our missions and our resources
- Striving to improve student success benchmarks via continuous quality improvement
- Serving as an integral part of the institutional master planning process
- Responding to external expectations and scrutiny of student outcomes

These pressures are exerted on an entire institution or system. Meeting the challenge of these pressures is not a laissez-faire process. These challenges cannot be met by one or two offices engaging in a marketing campaign, in changing registration processes, or in developing a new certificate program to boost completion rates. Executive leadership is required to pull together a comprehensive and coordinated vision and intentional plan to match mission with resources and with enrollment.

LEADERSHIP INGREDIENTS

While this chapter emphasizes the importance and value of executive leadership in SEM, it is essential to acknowledge that executive leadership alone is not the answer. The nature of the ingredients of leadership in SEM requires that they be exemplified by many throughout the organization.

Kurz (2003) outlines several ingredients that are useful to this discussion. He points out that leadership should be "fact-based" and "data driven." Thus offices around the college should be engaged in developing and using quality factual information to support the leadership in assessing strengths and weaknesses, opportunities, and challenges. Leadership should also have "knowledge and experience in higher education" particularly in understanding the interplay of mission and marketplace. Thirdly, leadership in SEM requires "collaboration." Integrating data with experience is a valuable outcome of collaboration, where the synergy of different perspectives produces not only data, but extends to analysis and the ability to prioritize and support those priorities in a coordinated and collaborative environment. Finally, Kurz suggests that leadership must be able to be "entrepreneurial" particularly in the face of uncertainties. Taking risks and being willing to experiment are sometimes the best responses to conflicting data and/or new trends that are difficult to assess.

Ward (2005) contributes two additional ingredients worth mentioning. She contends that leadership should demonstrate "commitment to vision and goals" and assure that campus culture embraces, as deeply as possible, an understanding and acceptance of the vision, mission, and goals of the college or system. Additionally, leadership should emphasize a collegial style of "communication." Asking probing questions, listening, synthesizing, and sharing information widely will support a college-wide buy-in to the leadership's direction.

Transformational leadership, as described by Northouse, is an important quality as well. It refers to "...the process whereby an individual engages with others and creates a connection that raises the level of motivation and morality in both the leader and the follower. This type of leader is attentive to the needs and motives of followers and tries to help followers reach their fullest potential (2001, p. 132).

Finally, we would like to suggest another ingredient. Leadership should have the ability to "think and plan strategically." We are faced with many competing challenges during this dawn of the twenty-first century. Separating the wheat from the chaff requires the data and the experience mentioned above, but also the willingness and ability to discover the opportunities and embark on strategic pathways to success.

Emphasis on data, marshalling the values of experience, collaboration and communication, embracing a common vision and goals, being willing to take risks when faced with uncertainties or new trends, and thinking strategically are certainly valuable ingredients. Is such a confluence of these remarkable ingredients possible? Sometimes not, but all is not lost if they are not immediately present. So it might be beneficial to add another ingredient—the value of incrementalism:

Leadership may need to "start small and build on success." Whether it is changing the direction of a very large ship [campus], or introducing change to a small campus entrenched in its ways, the introduction and implementation of enrollment management planning requires a delicate touch. In cases where the college is in some sort of desperate situation related to enrollment and the concomitant distressed finances, the development of enrollment management planning may be welcomed, though complicated to institute. In other cases, the visionaries of the college, faced with organizational barriers and/or enrollment complacency, may need to take steps where they can and incrementally build an infrastructure that will blossom at a later date (Kerlin 2004).

With these ingredients in mind, we are ready to start considering how to lead a SEM process.

BUILDING A LEADERSHIP APPROACH

Foremost, the president should set the stage by clarifying the value and importance of a healthy enrollment for the whole college. A healthy enrollment contributes to the strength of the college's financial balance sheet, to its capacity to roll with the punches, and to its ability to provide a positive atmosphere for professional development, quality programs, and services.

The president is a key contributor and overseer of a vibrant college-wide strategic plan and should assure that the strategic plan provides guideposts for enrollment planning. The president may be in the best position to monitor the alignment of the strategic vision and plan with the enrollment plan.

The president demonstrates that a healthy enrollment is everyone's business. By working with faculty leaders, the president emphasizes student success through appropriate program mix, relevant delivery modes and scheduling, and involvement with students. In working with administrative services, the president stresses efficient and usable business practices, well-kept facilities, accessible auxiliary services, and well-qualified human resources. The president also supports quality entry and retention services by working with student services, He assists college advancement, the foundation, and alumni with fundraising and friend-raising that augments the internal efforts of the college to support instructional programs and student services.

The president further promotes enrollment by including enrollment on cabinet level agendas as well as relevant administrative staff meetings, and emphasizing the role that recruitment, retention, and successful transfer/completion, plays within the institutional planning and budgeting cycles.

As the president determines the roles to be played by those who will facilitate a SEM process, he or she must also consider whether the mandate is one of strategic enrollment management or strategic enrollment leadership. Whiteside (1998) summarized the difference in the following manner: management's mandate is to minimize risk and keep the current system operating; and leadership's mandate is to implement change by creating a new system or way of doing things. Effective implementation of SEM generally requires the latter approach.

Though the president can and should develop an environment for a workable and inclusive method of developing enrollment strategies, the president is not the day-to-day planner and leader. As Theodore Roosevelt put it, "The best leader is the one who has sense enough to pick good people to do what he/she wants done, and self-restraint enough to keep from meddling with them while they do it."

Typically, community colleges utilize a committee approach, perhaps led by a specific vice-president or vice-presidential co-chairs. Some community colleges may create a "division" of enrollment management with a portfolio of those units often seen to be large influencers of enrollment, such as admissions and financial aid. The "right" way is whatever works best for the campus culture.

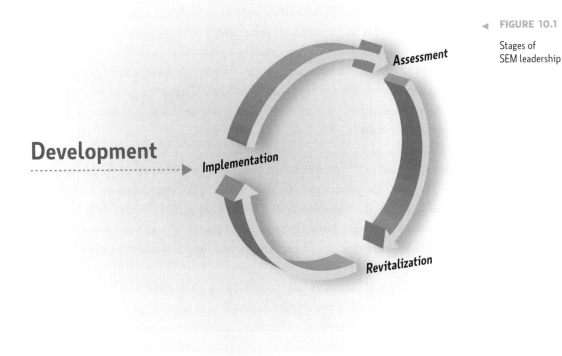

◀ **FIGURE 10.1**

Stages of
SEM leadership

No matter what the structure, the integration of all divisions of the college in the planning and implementation efforts is crucial. The president must provide a charge and continuously ask for information and accountability. The charge will lend clarity to those engaged in enrollment management. The call for accountability will keep the process lively.

LEADING SEM

It can be said that there are four stages to SEM leadership: 1) Development, 2) Implementation, 3) Assessment, and 4) Revitalization. In fact, after initial development, leading SEM is a circular process (*see* Figure 10.1, on page 175).

Development

As implied earlier, the development of strategic enrollment management relies heavily on executive buy-in and leadership to stress the value and purpose and establish a climate for planning. The actual development of a SEM approach will rely on a structure established by the leadership, be it a committee, a task force, or division.

Following on this, alignment with the college's strategic plan is critical. It is possible that a college without a vibrant strategic plan will have difficulty making positive strides in SEM, so in some cases it is wise to reestablish a strategic plan prior to engaging in SEM, though this could feel like a detour for those anxious to get started. Alignment with the strategic plan is one of the first challenges to those leading the SEM effort.

Additionally, SEM planning must be aligned and in many instances will drive the development and implementation of the college's master plan for facilities and campus lay-out. The master plan encompasses all planning documents for the college including the strategic plan as well as the SEM plan. However, SEM will play a pivotal role in a college's bond election, bond planning, and bond construction as well as campus infrastructure plans, in particular for states that require local taxpayers to vote on a bond levy.

With these basic factors in place, developing an approach to SEM and a plan can follow many or all of the aspects outlined in this book: gathering and analyzing data; identifying issues; and addressing technology, recruitment and retention, programs, and services. Such development should be done within an environment of input and communication throughout the college. This inclusive approach—one that recognizes that enrollment is everyone's business and builds strong partnerships—requires strong leadership that values collaboration. Zeiss makes a strong case for communication and collaboration that is relevant to strategic enrollment management. He reminds us that in doing so, we "eliminate the defensiveness and resistance" and enable ourselves to "discover new solutions" (2001, p. 80). Both of these notions bring value to the process of designing an institutional approach to strengthening enrollment.

Implementation

In an ideal world, a comprehensive SEM plan provides direction to various departments of the institution toward the goal of a healthy enrollment. The plan might include the specifics of implementation or might set overall goals that spur leaders and their staff to implement relevant activities.

In the real world, though, colleges might find themselves off to a less than perfect start. Data may have been difficult to find and analyze; campus technology may not fully support desired activities; some departments may not be fully on-board with enrollment management; or a limited budget may not support all that a plan envisions. Implementation, then, might be spotty or disjointed, or not institution-wide.

Frankly, either scenario is workable. Again, executive leadership comes into play. SEM rarely happens overnight, and it takes a steady "commitment to vision and goals" (Ward, 2005) and recognition that "incremental steps" (Kerlin 2004) may be the way a college will steadily progress toward its goals. Kouzes and Posner emphasize that sometimes "the most effective change processes are incremental " and that leaders can "help others see how progress can be made by breaking the journey down into measurable goals and milestones" (1995, pp. 243–244).

As the leadership seeks to implement its vision of SEM, perhaps the most significant action it can take is to assure coordination between the SEM planning activity and the budget cycle. While not every SEM strategy requires funding, there are certainly times when a realignment of resources, or an infusion of resources, can enable an institution to "turn the ship" and reach goals. Additionally, the long-term viability of SEM at any institution relies on the distribution of budget based on enrollment. A portion of division and departmental budgets, set and adjusted, based on the achievement of SEM goals via enrollment and retention, will ensure buy-in from institutional stakeholders.

As an institution moves to implementation of its enrollment management vision, constant communication with the whole campus is critical. Often a SEM approach kicks off with fanfare and highly visible meetings. As the hard work of actually analyzing data and developing plans goes on, however, those not directly involved may lose their connection to the value that SEM will play in institutional success. Leaders must constantly attend to keeping the message alive through various communication channels.

Assessment and Revitalization

Strategic enrollment management is always a work in progress. The chief reason for this, of course, is that the internal and external environments constantly shift and demand new responses. In addition, initial plans do not always have the expected outcomes. Thus, those who are leading SEM must build in a continuous or periodic assessment process and play a strong role in calling for reports and accountability.

Such assessment of the outcomes of plans and activities will provide much needed insight into how an institution is truly committed to SEM. In the early stages of SEM, it is easy to identify low-hanging fruit, or work with those who are most enthusiastic. Often the factors that can be most critical to the optimization of enrollment and its effect on the finances of the institution take a while to emerge.

It takes leadership talent and experience to use the assessment process to fully revitalize the SEM planning process. The lessons learned during initial development and implementation enable the institution to develop a more mature approach and more thoughtful strategies. For example, data analysis may improve to the point that more complex questions can be answered, or a more sophisticated understanding of revenue and expense may inform instructional program decisions. Kouzes and Posner draw a parallel with science, where major breakthroughs are likely to be the result of a series of earlier efforts (2001, p. 244).

CONCLUSION

In the end, if the president has set the stage effectively, the president has the easy roles—that of visionary, architect, coach, supporter, and/or cheerleader, as well as confessor from time to time. The hard work goes to the leaders who sit on committees, who write plans, who crunch and analyze data, who implement services, who transform programs, who make progress reports, and who engage in the assessment and revitalization of continuous enrollment management. Leadership skills in communication and collaboration—and the ability to stay committed to the vision and goals—are the hallmarks of success in SEM.

IMPLEMENTING SEM AT THE
Community College

by *Bob Bontrager* and Alicia Moore

11

For the purposes of this book, strategic enrollment management is defined as *a concept and process that enables the fulfill-ment of institutional mission and students' educational goals.* Building from this basic definition, the conceptual part of SEM can be described as an institution's overall alignment with regard to its enrollment goals. Achieving such alignment is a complex undertaking that requires multiphase planning and implementation, with multiple planning models having been suggested (Kerlin 2008; Bontrager 2008).

Figure 11.1 (on page 184) illustrates the concept of SEM alignment.

While not entirely hierarchical or linear, the components represented in this diagram can be used to assess both the current state of enrollment efforts, as well as to identify potential next steps for further developing the SEM organization, capabilities of, and outcomes within an institution. As an institution engages in enrollment planning, it is best to begin at the base of the pyramid and work up.

Adopting a SEM approach takes discipline. Because the will to implement SEM often results from significant enrollment concerns, typically it is accompanied by a sense of urgency. For this reason, there is a strong temptation to skip over the first three foundational planning stages—which are time consuming and require their own resources—and go directly to strategies and tactics. Unfortunately, there are no short cuts. Implementing enrollment strategies and tactics without adequate pre-planning will, at best, result in short term enrollment gains. Moreover, the "quick fix" approach is more costly than necessary, in terms of both direct costs and staff time. Institutions are better served by devoting the time and resources necessary to

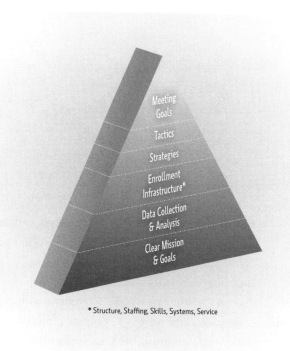

FIGURE 11.1 ▶

SEM Planning
Framework

Meeting
Goals

Tactics

Strategies

Enrollment
Infrastructure*

Data Collection
& Analysis

Clear Mission
& Goals

* Structure, Staffing, Skills, Systems, Service

gain campus-wide understanding and buy-in relative to enrollment goals, based on hard data and with a clear plan for establishing the infrastructure needed to support any anticipated change in enrollment outcomes.

CLEAR MISSION AND GOALS

Many institutions develop their enrollment goals based on a simple model: they look to last year's enrollment and project incremental changes—in the number or profile of students—for the next one or two years. The magnitude of the projected changes generally is determined by budget considerations or external measures of success such as state mandates or community needs. When finances are the primary driver, the enrollment target rises or falls based on the amount of tuition revenue needed to achieve the desired budget outcome.

There are a number of limitations to this basic approach. It creates a short-term planning mindset that looks backward to prior performance, rather than forward to a desired future. It fails to account for the longer time period required for specific recruitment and retention strategies to take hold and achieve the desired results. It fails to account for the range of investments and costs associated with recruiting and retaining different types of students, leaving open the very real possibility that the institution meets its enrollment goals, but ends up losing money. Finally, it focuses on enrollment as a number, usually as a single aggregate number, rather than establishing multiple goals for different types of students. As a result, institutions can too easily lose sight of desired outcomes other than budgetary, including goals for access, equity, and student success.

Effective SEM planning begins with the creation of mission-driven enrollment goals. These include a goal for total enrollment and, more importantly, goals for the types of students and the proportion of students within each type that would best fulfill the institution's mission. The very process of developing such goals can quickly reveal different perceptions of the institution's mission among various campus stakeholders. In those cases, SEM has proven to be a useful framework for clarifying mission understandings. Another benefit of the goal-setting process is shifting stakeholders to a forward-looking, long-term planning mode, toward a desired future for the institution. This itself has proven to be a powerfully positive force for institutions that adopt a SEM approach to planning (Bontrager, Brown, and Hossler 2008).

DATA COLLECTION AND ANALYSIS

Data is central to the SEM planning process and a necessary component of each planning stage. While referred to in a variety of ways—performance indicators, success indicators, and outcomes assessment to name a few—SEM relies on a broad array of metrics to assess the achievement of goals, evaluate program effectiveness, and benchmark operations and strategies with other institutions.

This book includes a chapter on the data driven nature of SEM, and the many pertinent points made there will not be repeated here; however, two common pitfalls will be emphasized. One is the overreliance on anecdotal data, with decision making relegated to an exchange of one-off student experiences that are repeated as generalized conclusions. In these cases, decisions tend to be made on the basis of the anecdote offered by the highest ranking person in the discussion. The second common pitfall is to collect copious amounts of data, but to fail to conduct adequate analysis to make it useful in decision making. Suffice it to say that the prominent, foundational position of this component in the SEM Planning Diagram is completely deliberate and speaks to importance of data in making SEM work.

ENROLLMENT INFRASTRUCTURE

Implementing SEM requires attention to a number of interrelated infrastructure issues. Some of these, such as staffing and systems issues, seem less tangible in their influence on enrollment and therefore often receive less attention and resources than they deserve. The temptation is to skip past them in favor of strategies and tactics that appear—superficially—to have a greater impact on enrollment outcomes. A brief description of each of the infrastructure subcomponents follows.

Structure refers to the organizational structure of the college. There are no hard and fast rules about the "right" organizational structure for SEM. On the one hand, many institutions have found it beneficial to bring together key enrollment service functions into a single administrative division. Basic SEM divisions within a college typically include outreach, admissions, records, financial aid, and testing. More complex SEM organizations may include additional functions such as orientation, academic support, and international student services. Ultimately, what matters in terms of making SEM work is not moving boxes around on an organizational chart, but rather the extent to which departments and functions work together to achieve commonly understood enrollment goals.

STAFFING focuses on the efficient deployment of staff resources. Staff may be added to certain departments when enrollment increases or specialized service needs, for example, responding to e-mail queries, outstrip available staff time. A SEM approach may also result in staff reductions, as efficiencies are gained via streamlined business practices or technology implementation. Finally, staff may be reassigned, as the time required to complete certain tasks changes, usually through shifting service needs and technology enhancements. An example of reassignment for many colleges is the decreased need for staff in the records area, where technology has eliminated many processes that previously were manual and more time consuming. At the same time, community colleges recruit students now in ways that would not have existed ten to fifteen years ago, requiring the addition of recruitment staff when previously none were needed.

● **SKILLS** are closely related to staffing issues, involving the extent to which existing staff possess the skills required of leading-edge SEM practices. The most common examples relate to technology, where clerical functions previously reliant on hard-copy documents are now more often completed electronically. Another example is recruitment, which previously relied heavily on in-person presence at high schools and college fairs, and now is driven to a much greater extent by web and e-mail communications. At four-year institutions, the latter shift has led many institutions to recast traditional admission counselor roles as information or communication specialists, with skills in online media. Such a change can be expected in the two-year sector as well.

● **SYSTEMS** refer to the delivery of efficient and effective enrollment services, representing students' gateway to the college. This is true both at the point of initial enrollment as well as throughout a student's tenure with the institution. A college may offer relevant and competitive academic programs; however, if students encounter difficulty in acquiring information, completing transactions, registering for classes, accessing financial aid, and so forth, they are less likely to enroll initially and less likely to stay enrolled. Efficiency and effectiveness of systems results from coordination along four dimensions.

▶ *Strategy*: this involves a college's overall SEM strategy, as well sub-strategies that address recruitment, retention, communications, and marketing.

▶ *Policy*: this includes academic and administrative policies that provide guidance to effective business practices, *e.g.*, placement testing policies, course prerequisites, and criteria for admission to or continuation in specific programs.

▶ *Practice*: this involves the way policies are carried out in the business practices that facilitate transactions with students and among campus departments, including workflow and process mapping, *e.g.*, procedures for responding to inquiries from prospective students, processing financial aid, and registration procedures.

▶ *Technology*: this includes the implementation of policy and practice through the use of technology.

FIGURE 11.2 ▶

Creating Effective
SEM Systems

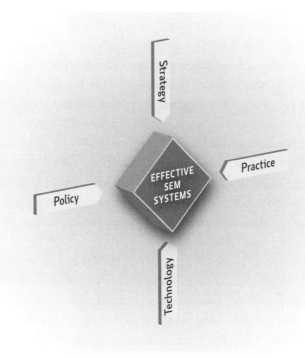

The interplay of these areas is illustrated in Figure 11.2.

● **SERVICE** is the summary aspect of enrollment infrastructure, representing the extent to which an institution meets students' wants and needs, *as students define them*. Few would argue the merits of this approach, but doing so is more difficult than it sounds. Institutional history and precedent is powerful; the explanation of "this is how we have always done it" is all too tempting. While such an approach has always had its limitations, it is especially debilitating in the current technology-driven environment, in which leading-edge initiatives are quickly outdated. In this context, continuous tracking and response to data on the student experience is more vital than ever.

Infrastructures of all types are commonly overlooked. No news is good news—until the plumbing springs a leak or the electricity goes off! Similarly, it can be difficult to attract attention to issues of enrollment infrastructure. That will not be the case when the registration system crashes at the start of fall term or when financial aid is not dispersed in a timely manner. However, systems deficiencies as they relate to SEM tend to be more insidious. Shortcomings typically manifest themselves in the form of seemingly minor glitches as students seek to complete enrollment transactions. It may not seem problematic to require a student to complete an additional step for admission to a program, unless the individual is a first-generation attender or has personal challenges that make the extra step the one that causes them to walk away entirely. In these days of multiple options for gaining access to higher education courses and programs, students of all types will compare one institution to another and will be inclined to choose the institution that provides them the clearest pathway to achieving their educational goal.

The importance of a competitive enrollment infrastructure is reinforced by this reality: for many institutions, infrastructure enhancements pose the greatest opportunity to realize near-term improvement in enrollment outcomes. That reality is belied by the tendency of most institutions to give far greater attention to strategies and tactics in the pursuit of enrollment goals. Given the predominant focus on strategies and tactics in professional presentations and literature, they will not be revisited here. Rather, the remainder of this chapter will be devoted to a case study that illustrates the translation of the preceding theoretical constructs into actual implementation at a community college.

IMPLEMENTING SEM: A CASE STUDY

In winter 2007, Central Oregon Community College (COCC) embarked on an ambitious path to develop a comprehensive strategic enrollment management plan using the SEM Planning Framework reviewed in this chapter. The college hoped to complete the plan within six months, despite having to start from scratch. Just over two years later, the COCC SEM team has a working draft of institutional enrollment goals, has finalized the data review supporting those goals, and is ready to embark on the next aspect of strategic enrollment management, that of institutionalizing the SEM plan. This case study shares highlights of COCC's SEM journey and the recommendations to make this process successful at other institutions.

Central Oregon Community College is a two-year institution located in one of the fastest growing communities in the region, serving a ten-thousand-square mile college district. It represents a typical community college, offering a balance of transfer and career/technical education majors; its students are primarily commuter students (although the campus offers a small residence hall), with an average age of twenty-five and a sixty/forty split of women and men; its revenue streams are a balance of state dollars, tuition/fees, and local property taxes; and its enrollment goals are based on annual budgetary needs. However, there are two aspects that make COCC unique in comparison to many peer institutions:

- From 1995 to 2005, the COCC district grew from 127,751 to 175,713 (1,276 percent increase) citizens, while the institution's overall credit and noncredit headcount decreased by 7.4 percent during the same time frame.

- The college is located in one of the premier outdoor recreation locations in the Pacific Northwest, making it an attractive option to its nearly 17 percent non-resident students.

The need for more definitive direction on both of these components, as well as unstable revenue sources, spurred institutional momentum towards development of a comprehensive SEM plan to guide future objectives.

Setting the Stage

Setting the stage—that is, garnering buy-in at all levels of the institution and developing a common understanding of the purpose and outcomes of a SEM plan—is perhaps the most critical aspect of any strategic enrollment management process. At COCC, constantly fluctuating and unpredictable enrollment growth and its associated affect on the campus budget generated institution-wide discussions regarding how better to predict enrollment and the importance of cross-campus support. Seizing the opportunity, COCC's enrollment leaders frequently discussed the topic of SEM in a variety of campus committees and eventually adopted a survey method to establish SEM in the forefront of everyone's thinking and assess the institution's readiness to embark on a formal SEM planning process.

The audit survey was administered to the campus executive team, instructional leadership, all academic department chairs, all administrative department direc-

Rank your institution in the dimensions of SEM listed below.

Poor ---------------------------- Excellent

	Poor				Excellent	
1. Clarity of institutional mission	①	②	③	④	⑤	N/A
2. Alignment of institutional mission and enrollment goals	①	②	③	④	⑤	N/A
3. Specific enrollment targets based on:						
Total enrollment	①	②	③	④	⑤	N/A
Student academic ability	①	②	③	④	⑤	N/A
Ethnicity	①	②	③	④	⑤	N/A
Geographic origin	①	②	③	④	⑤	N/A
Academic major	①	②	③	④	⑤	N/A
Undergraduate/graduate level	①	②	③	④	⑤	N/A
Other:	①	②	③	④	⑤	N/A
4. SEM participation and buy-in from:						
Top-level administrators	①	②	③	④	⑤	N/A
Academic colleges and departments	①	②	③	④	⑤	N/A
Student service departments	①	②	③	④	⑤	N/A
Multicultural programs	①	②	③	④	⑤	N/A
Campus community as a whole	①	②	③	④	⑤	N/A
5. Use of financial aid in promoting enrollment goals	①	②	③	④	⑤	N/A
6. Coordination of enrollment goals with institutional budget planning	①	②	③	④	⑤	N/A
7. Strategic allocation of funds to support enrollment goals	①	②	③	④	⑤	N/A
8. Institutional research:						
Amount of relevant data available	①	②	③	④	⑤	N/A
Campus distribution of enrollment data	①	②	③	④	⑤	N/A
Use of enrollment data in campus decision making	①	②	③	④	⑤	N/A

◀ FIGURE 11.3

Central Oregon
Community College
SEM Audit

ADAPTED FROM
BONTRAGER 2007

tors, and all enrollment and student services managers, thereby generating common talking points amongst the campus' formal and informal leadership teams. It identified the institution's strengths (leadership support for strategic planning, availability of data to support the planning process, clarity of institutional mission, and positive relationships/trust between instruction and enrollment services). More importantly, the survey clearly identified the institution's weakness: without exception, all groups agreed that the college did not have commonly accepted enrollment goals. While the survey itself was a means of starting the discussion, the results were the final impetus needed to launch a formal SEM planning process.

Enrollment leadership researched a variety of SEM planning models and chose to adopt the planning framework outlined at the beginning of this chapter. As the aforementioned survey results were shared with various groups, so too, was this model. Across the board, groups embraced the concept and the college was ready to start the formal SEM planning process.

Establishing a SEM Team

While establishing campus buy-in is critical, so too is who helps lead the SEM planning process. Some would posit that the institution's executive leadership team (*e.g.,* president's cabinet) should be the group leading the SEM process, and this may be true at some institutions. However, letting campus culture determine the best approach to the process is an important consideration. At COCC, this meant having active support from its executive team, but allowing a variety of campus individuals to participate in and develop the plan. With this, the dean of student and enrollment services and director of college relations (both members of the campus executive team) were asked to co-chair the SEM planning process, as the two had a longstanding positive working relationship and a strong level of support from a variety of campus groups. Additionally, in order to keep the conversation alive at all levels and in all divisions of the institution, a cross-campus team was formed. The COCC SEM team consisted of instructional representatives (dean of credit instruction, dean of noncredit instruction, transfer faculty, career/technical education faculty), student services (admissions, registrar, financial aid, academic advising), institutional research, associate chief financial officer, and the vice president for institutional advancement (with responsibilities for technology and the college's foundation, and a member of the campus executive team). Individuals were not only chosen due to their areas of responsibility and connection to possible SEM goals and strategies, but also because they were seen as both formal and informal leaders in a variety of campus settings.

In developing the SEM Team, the co-chairs realized that while the group represented nearly all aspects of the campus, they also brought different levels of understanding of not only SEM, but of COCC's enrollment history and variety of credit and noncredit programs. Significant time—as much as six months—was spent teaching COCC's SEM model to the team and providing appropriate (but not overwhelming) SEM research. These six months were likewise spent understanding COCC's enrollment history at all levels, including non-credit enrollment and programs. Through these discussions, two primary outcomes emerged that served as our foundation throughout the planning process:

- The SEM team committed to developing a comprehensive enrollment management plan, one that included both credit and noncredit goals (COCC noncredit programs are defined as adult basic education, English language learners, community learning, business development and employee/workforce training), as noncredit participants represented 56 percent of the institution's overall headcount and are fundamental to the mission of community colleges.
- The SEM team developed the COCC strategic enrollment management core concepts, which served as a guide throughout the planning process. The team's core concepts were:
  - ▶ *Students,* and their success, are at the core of all that we do.
  - ▶ SEM goals will align with the institution's *mission* and goal statements.
  - ▶ *Participation* from across the campus is critical to an institution's ability to meet goals set forth in a SEM plan. As such, no single person is responsible for achieving the goals set forth in this plan; rather, collaboration amongst and coordination between all levels of the campus is critical to success.
  - ▶ Attention will be given to the *fiscal impact* of SEM goals and associated plans to achieve those goals before the goal is finalized.
  - ▶ *Relevant data* will be collected and used when setting institutional enrollment goals and assessing strategies and tactics.

Clear Mission and Goals

During the review of COCC's enrollment history and institutional programs, a few key questions about current trends, their affect on enrollment, and their alignment with institutional mission emerged. If having a clear institutional mission is a critical aspect of the SEM process, then understanding and support from the group responsible for setting institutional mission is needed as well. At COCC, this is the institution's board of directors. Using this opportunity, the SEM team presented a brief SEM overview to the board and asked them to clarify the institutional mission in light of the questions raised. Doing so not only resulted in the board of directors reaffirming the institution's mission and providing clear direction to the development of specific goals, but also provided an opportunity to engage the board with the SEM process.

With the institutional mission reaffirmed by the board of directors, the SEM team developed four primary goal themes:

- Enrollment, Recruiting, and Outreach
- Persistence and Graduation Rates
- Access and Affordability
- Credit and Non-Credit Offerings

Data Review and Goal Development

Data, data, and more data - It could have been overwhelming, but given the commitment to COCC's core concept of only reviewing relevant data, the SEM team limited its review to critical data points to further refine institutional enrollment goals. In doing so, the team avoided "interesting data," that is, anything that began with the statement "it would be nice to know...." With this, they asked the following guiding questions in determining relevant data points:

- What data elements are critical to understanding the four goal areas?
- What current trends, albeit within or out of institutional control, are shaping the four enrollment goal/theme areas?
- What questions has the institution politely avoided, but which may affect the SEM goal/theme areas?
- What issues need to be set aside and addressed by future SEM teams?

Answering these questions allowed the team to move in a forward direction, instead of spending potentially years and years mired in a data review. From these findings, the team developed a series of data conclusions, along with each of the four goal areas, to share with the campus. The SEM team co-chairs and individual team members met with a variety of campus groups (*e.g.*, board of directors, academic department chairs, administrative department directors, individual student support areas, instructional leadership, and more) to gauge the campus' general reaction. Although many were surprised at the findings, all agreed that they represented the appropriate direction for the college and supported the initial goal areas. While by no means complete, the following data conclusions were the most eye opening for the campus:

- *Part-Time Attendance:* More credit students are attending COCC part-time, with only 13.5 percent of the 2005–06 enrollment attending full-time over the course of an academic year (940 of 6,969 students). However, few program offerings are structured to accommodate part-timers.
- *Credit and Noncredit Headcount and FTE:* Fifty-seven percent of total COCC headcount are students taking non-credit classes (includes all non-credit offerings), while 85 percent of total FTE is generated through credit offerings.
- *Non-Resident Headcount:* Between 2001–02 and 2006–07, the number of non-resident students has more than doubled, from 536 (7.2 percent of enrollment) to 1,136 (16 percent).
- *Gift Aid and Loans:* Gift aid comprised 46 percent of a student's total financial aid package in 2001–02, while loans made up 54 percent. In 2006–07, gift aid dropped to 40 percent, while loans increased to 60 percent.
- *College Preparedness:* Over the last six years, 18 percent of first-time freshman tested into college-level math and writing, with 77 percent successful their first term; 35 percent tested in college-level writing or math, with 66 percent successful their first term; and 47 percent tested in to developmental/pre-100 level in writing and math, with 58 percent successful their first term.
- *High School Programs:* Early indicators suggest that 35 percent of students who participate in a college class while in a high school program later attend COCC.

The SEM team then broke into four groups based on areas of interest and potential to impact the goal strategies, with each team member serving on two sub-teams. The primary roles of sub-teams involved developing the specifics behind each goal and reviewing additional relevant data to support the goal's recommended direction. The sub-teams brought their recommendations to the full SEM team for review, solicited feedback from campus departments and committees, and eventually brought recommendations to the executive team for approval. Interestingly enough, the time spent developing a common understanding of SEM concepts, institutional programs, and institutional enrollment history, as well as providing continuous feedback to the campus, took approximately fifteen months. Such upfront preparation, however, paid dividends in the end, as construction and approval of the goal specifics took just two months.

Enrollment Infrastructure

With the long-term goals set, questions arose as to how to maintain the forward momentum, how to ensure that the right individuals were part of the infrastructure review and implementation process, and how to continue to involve the full campus. To this end, COCC adopted the SEM organizational structure shown in Table 11.1 (on page 197), based loosely on a model from California State University–Pomona (Freer 2008).

Summary Comments

As mentioned at the beginning of this case study, the Central Oregon Community College SEM team planned on having a full SEM plan on the ground within six months of the team's inception. However, it took nearly two years to obtain fully-developed enrollment goals. Was the time spent worth it? Absolutely, and while the outcomes cannot be yet fully measured, the results of this thoughtful, strategic process meant that the College now had data-driven, student-oriented goals and that a platform for long-term, intentional growth was in place. Most importantly, all levels of the institution—including the board of directors, campus executive team, faculty and staff—understood and embraced the value of SEM. That, in and of itself, is success.

CONCLUSION

If the purposes of SEM include such things as establishing comprehensive goals, promoting students' academic success, creating a data-rich environment, and strengthening communications and marketing, clearly SEM at community colleges faces many challenges. However, as the saying goes, with challenge comes opportunity. Though it will not be easy, the breadth and depth of issues represented by the current state

**TABLE II.I. CENTRAL OREGON COMMUNITY COLLEGE
SEM ORGANIZATIONAL STRUCTURE**

Team Members	Responsibilities
STRATEGIC ENROLLMENT MANAGEMENT LEADERSHIP TEAM	
■ President ■ Vice President of Instruction ■ Vice President of Administration ■ Chief Financial Officer ■ Dean of Student & Enrollment Services ■ Director of College Relations	■ Review progress towards annual SEM goals ■ Approve new SEM goals/direction ■ Consider SEM goals in budget allocations ■ One to two regular executive team meetings per quarter to focus solely on SEM updates and issues
STRATEGIC ENROLLMENT MANAGEMENT COORDINATING TEAM (Recommends to SEM Leadership Team)	
■ Instructional Dean ■ Associate Chief Financial Officer ■ Director of Admissions/Registrar ■ Director of Financial Aid ■ Director, CAP (Career, Academic, & Personal Counseling) Center ■ Chair, Faculty Council ■ Institutional Research Coordinator	■ Develop annual SEM report, including recommendations for new or changing goals ■ Recommend strategies for reaching SEM goals (including those from task force teams and/or SEM coordinating team) ■ Recommend a predictive analysis model for enrollment projections, recruitment targets, retention, and student success factors ■ Recommend enrollment assumptions for budget planning purposes ■ Coordinate and provide direction for SEM task force teams ■ Meet regularly throughout quarter
STRATEGIC ENROLLMENT MANAGEMENT: TOPIC-SPECIFIC TASK FORCES (Reports to SEM Coordinating Team)	
■ Four volunteers from across campus chosen based on topic and areas of interest ■ One member of SEM coordinating team	■ Each task force to focus on one SEM goal/topic area ■ Research and develop strategies to reach SEM goals (fall and winter quarters) ■ Recommend strategies to SEM coordinating team (spring quarter) ■ Meet every two weeks; support to come from SEM coordinating team member

of higher education in the United States—as well as other countries—offers a prime opportunity to rethink the way ahead for community colleges. This book does not provide all the answers for making the transition, but instead sets us on the path for addressing the multiplicity of issues, thereby moving SEM forward in community colleges toward the ultimate goals of institutional vitality and student success.

REFERENCES

Adelman, C. 1989. *Using transcripts to validate institutional mission: The role of the community college in the postsecondary experience of a generation.* Paper presented at the Annual Meeting of the Association for the Study of Higher Education, November, Atlanta, GA.

———. 2000. *More Than 13 Ways of Looking at Degree Attainment.* Trenton, NJ: New Jersey State Department of Higher Education, Office of Community College Programs. ERIC Document Reproduction Service No. ED455875.

———. 2007a. Learning without borders: Training a global workforce requires international collaboration. *Community College Journal.* 78(3): 28–30.

———. 2007b. *Building a Culture of Transfer.* Slide presentation published July 30. Washington, DC: Institute for Higher Education Policy. Available at: <www.ihep.org/assets/files/staff-presentations/TRANSFER CONF.ppt>.

Allison, D.H, and A.D. DeBlois. 2008. Current Issues Survey Report, 2008. *Educause Quarterly.* 31(2): 14–30. Available at: <www.educause.edu/ir/library/pdf/eqm0823.pdf>.

"Ameriwire" (User's Screen Name). 2004.: *The plural of anecdote is not data* (August 13 forum posting). *Everything2.com.* Retrieved April 23, 2009 from: <http://everything2.com/index.pl?node_id=163824>.

Anderson, P. 2007. *What is the Web 2.0? Ideas, Technologies and Implications for Education.* JISC Technlogy and Standards Watch report. Bristol, UK: Joint Information Systems Committee.

Arizona Board of Regents. 2004. *Redesigning Arizona's University System.* Executive Summary from Arizona Board of Regents' June 3, 2004 meeting. Retrieved April 1, 2007 from <www.abor.asu.edu/special_editions/redesign/SPBDmtg%20603exec%20sum%20reorg.pdf>.

Arnold, J.C. 2001. Student transfer between Oregon community colleges and Oregon university system institutions. *New Directions for Community Colleges.* 114: 45–59.

Balzer, J.L. 2006. *Community College and University Degree Partnership Programs: A Qualitative Study of the Student Experience.* Unpublished doctoral dissertation, Oregon State University, Corvallis, Oregon.

Barnes, N. 2009. E-mail correspondence. (W. Kilgore, Interviewer). May 6.

Barnes, N.G., and E. Mattson. 2009. *Social Media and College Admissions: The First Longitudinal Study.* University of Massachusetts Dartmouth Center for Marketing Research.

Barr, M.J. 2002. *Jossey-Bass Academic Administrator's Guide to Budgets and Financial Management.* San Francisco: Wiley.

Basken, P. 2008. 2-year colleges are eager to prove their worth. *The Chronicle of Higher Education.* Retrieved from: <http://chronicle.com/daily/2008/10/5612.n.htm>.

Baumol, W.J., and W.G. Bowen. 1966. *Performing Arts, the Economic Dilemma; A Study of Problems Common to Theater, Opera, Music, and Dance.* New York: The Twentieth Century Fund.

The Benchmarking Exchange. 2009. *What is Benchmarking* (web page)? Aptos, CA: TBE. Retrieved May 15, 2009 from: <www.benchnet.com/wib.htm>.

Black, Jim. 2004. Integrated college and university marketing. In *Student Marketing for Colleges and Universities*, edited by R. Whiteside. Washington, DC: American Association of Collegiate Registrar and Admissions Officers.

Boggs, G.R., and M.B. Seltzer. 2008. What to measure and reward at community colleges. *Inside Higher Ed.* February 25, Views section. Available at: <www.insidehighered.com/views/2008/02/25/boggs>.

Bontrager, B. 2004a. Enrollment management: An introduction to concepts and structure. *College and University.* 79(3): 11–16.

———. 2004b. *The Student Success Continuum.* Paper presented at Oregon Association of Collegiate Registrars and Admissions Officers, May 2–4, Ashland, Oregon.

———. 2007. *Institutional SEM Audit.* Unpublished document.

———. 2008. *SEM and Institutional Success: Integrating Enrollment, Finance and Student Access.* Washington, DC: American Association of Collegiate Registrar and Admissions Officers.

Bontrager, B. and G. Brown. 2008. Integrating enrollment and budget planning: The SEM planning model. In *SEM and Institutional Success*, edited by B. Bontrager. Washington, DC: The American Association of Collegiate Registrars and Admissions Officers.

Bontrager, B., B. Clemetsen, and T. Watts. 2005. A community college/university dual enrollment program. *College and University.* 80(4): 3–6.

Bowen, W.G. 1973. *Higher education: who pays? Who benefits? Who should pay? A report and recommendations.* New York: McGraw-Hill.

———. 1980. *The Costs of Higher Education: How Much Do Colleges and Universities Spend Per Student and How Much Should They Spend?* San Francisco: Jossey-Bass.

Cejda, B.D. 1999. The role of the community college in baccalaureate attainment at a private liberal arts college. *Community College Review.* 99(7): 1–13.

Cejda, B.D., and A. Kaylor. 2001. Early transfer: A case study of traditional-aged community college students. *Community College Journal of Research and Practice.* 25: 621–638.

Center for Community College Student Engagement. 2006. *Act on Fact: Using Data to Improve Student Success* (2006 CCSSE findings). Austin, TX: The University of Texas Austin, Community College Leadership Program.

———. 2008. *Imagine Success: Engaging Entering Students* (2008 SENSE filed test findings). Austin, TX.: The University of Texas Austin, Community College Leadership Program.

Clemetsen, B. and J.L. Balzer. 2008. Community college and university degree partnerships: Paving the path to success. *College and University.* 83(3): 12–19.

Cohen, A.M. and F. Brawer. 2003. *The American Community College.* San Francisco: Jossey-Bass.

Corliss, R. 2009. *How to Monitor Your Social Media Presence in 10 Minutes a Day.* April 8. Retrieved April 26 from: <http://blog.hubspot.com/blog/tabid/6307/bid/4663/How-to-Monitor-Your-Social-Media-Presence-in-10-Minutes-a-Day.aspx>.

Culver, T. 2008. *A New Way to Measure Student Success* (white paper). Coralville, IA: Noel Levitz. Available at: <www.noellevitz.com/NR/rdonlyres/924F9D03-5CBB-4C06-B8BA-B1EACA11D3C7/0/StudentSuccessFunnel08.pdf>

De Los Santos, A.G., and I. Wright. 1990. Maricopa's swirling students: Earning one third of Arizona State's bachelor's degrees. *Community, Technical, and Junior College Journal.* 60(6): 32–34.

Deutsch, P.J. 2008. *Admissions 101.* Presentation at Ohio ACRAO. Retrieved June 2, 2009 from: <www.oacac.org/attachments/admissions%20101.SI04.ppt>.

Dolence, M.G. 1993. *A Primer for Campus Administrators.* Washington, D.C.: American Association of Collegiate Registrars and Admissions Officers.

———. 1998. *The ABCs of Strategic Enrollment Management.* PowerPoint presentation SEM VII Conference. Aspen, CO.

Dougherty, H. 2009. Twitter catches up to Digg. *Hitwise Intelligence—Analyst Blogs.* January 20. Retrieved April 25, 2009 from: <http://weblogs.hitwise.com/heather-dougherty/2009/01/twitter_catches_up_to_digg.html>.

Ewell, P. 2007. *Community College Bridges to Opportunity Initiative: Joint State Data Toolkit.* Austin, TX: Bridges to Opportunity Initiative and Community College Leadership Program, University of Texas at Austin.

Findly Schenck, B., and L. English. 2001. *Small Business Marketing for Dummies.* New York: Hungry Minds, Inc. Publishers.

Finnegan, C.L., K.A. Webb, and L.V. Morris. 2007. *Technology in the College Admission Process: Impact on Process, Professionals and Institutions.* Alexandria, VA: National Association for College Admission Counseling.

Freer, Doug and K. Street. 2008. *Engaging the Campus in Enrollment Management and Student Success.* Presentation from the 2008 AACRAO Strategic Enrollment Management Conference. Los Angeles, CA.

Frommer, D. 2009. U.S. Airways crash rescue picture: Citizen journalism, Twitter at work. *The Business Insider.* January 15, Silicon Alley Insider section. Retrieved April 16, 2009 from: <www.businessinsider. com/2009/1/us-airways-crash-rescue-picture-citizen-jouralism-twitter-at-work>.

Glenn, R. 2008. *Shared Enrollment Services as a Potential SEM Strategy.* American Association of Collegiate Registrars and Admissions Officers SEM Conference, Anaheim, CA.

Google. 2009. *Google Alerts* (service home page). Retrieved September 3 from: <www.google.com/alerts>.

Habley, W.R., and J.L. Bloom. 2007. Giving advice that makes a difference. In *Fostering Student Success in the Campus Community,* edited by G.L. Kramer and Associates. San Francisco: Jossey-Bass.

Harbin, C.E. 1997. A survey of transfer students at four-year institutions serving a California community college. *Community College Review.* 25(2): 21–40.

Henderson, S.E. 2005. Refocusing SEM. Losing structure and finding the academic context. *College and University.* 80(3): 3–8.

Hossler, D, and D.H. Kalsbeek. 2008. Enrollment management and managing enrollment: Setting the context for dialogue. *College and University.* 83(4): 3–9.

IANA. *See* Internet Assigned Numbers Authority.

Internet Assigned Numbers Authority . 2009. *Country-Code Top Level Domains.* Retrieved May 13 from: <www.iana.org/domains/root/cctld/>.

Jaschik, S. 2007. Challenging the measures of success. *Inside Higher Ed.* June 6. Available at: <www.insidehigher ed.com/news/2007/06/06/rates>.

———. 2008. Alternative measure of success. *Inside Higher Ed.* October 22. Available at: <www.insidehigher ed.com/news/2008/10/22/alaska >.

Johnson, K. 2006. *Portland Community College's Communication Plan.* Personal communication.

Kalsbeek, D. 2006a. Some reflections on SEM structures and strategies (part one). *College and University.* 81(3) 3–10.

———. 2006b. Some reflections on SEM structures and strategies (part two). *College and University.* 81(4) 3–10.

Kalsbeek, D., and D. Hossler. 2009. Enrollment management—A market-centered perspective. *College and University.* 84(3): 2–11.

Kearney, G.W. 1995. Multiple-transfer students in a public urban university: Background characteristics and interinstitutional movements. *Research in Higher Education.* 36(3): 323–344.

Keller, J. 2007a. Virginia lawmakers consider bill to encourage students to start at 2-year colleges. The *Chronicle of Higher Education.* 53(21): A22.

Keller, M.J. 2007b. *Development of Statewide Community College Value-Added Accountability Measures.* Paper presented at SHEEO/NCES Network Conference, St. Petersburg, FL. May 9.

Kerlin, C. 2004. *Essentials of Enrollment Management: Cases in the Field.* Washington DC: American Association of Collegiate Registrars and Admissions Officers.

———. 2008. A community college roadmap for the enrollment management journey. *College and University.* (83)4: 10–14.

King, M.C., and R.N. Fox. 2007. Achieving student success in two-year colleges. In *Fostering Student Success in the Campus Community,* edited by G.L. Kramer and Associates. San Francisco: Jossey-Bass.

Kintzer, F.C., and J.L. Wattenbarger. 1985. *The Articulation/Transfer Phenomenon: Patterns and Directions.* Washington, DC: American Association of Community and Junior Colleges.

Kinzie, J., and G.D. Kuh. 2007. Creating a student-centered culture. In *Fostering Student Success in the Campus Community*, edited by G.L. Kramer and Associates. San Francisco: Jossey-Bass.

Kisker, C.B. 2007. Creating and sustaining community college–university transfer partnerships. *Community College Review.* 34(4): 282–301.

Knapp, L.G., J.E. Kelly-Reid, and S.A. Ginder. 2009. *Enrollment in Postsecondary Institutions, Fall 2007; Graduation Rates, 2001 and 2004 Cohorts; and Financial Statistics, Fiscal Year 2007* (NCES Publication No. 2009155). Washington, DC: National Center for Education Statistics. Available at: <http://nces.ed.gov/pubs2009/2009155.pdf>.

Kouzes, J.M., and B.Z. Posner. 1995. *The Leadership Challenge.* San Francisco: Jossey-Bass.

Kurz, K. 2003. Profile of an effective enrollment manager. *College and University.* 79(2): 39–41.

League for Innovation in the Community College. 2009. *Academic Master Planning* (Web page). Retrieved May 29 from: <www.league.org/services/Academic_Planning.html>.

Leinbach, T.D., and D. Jenkins. 2008. Using longitudinal data to increase community college student success: A guide to measuring milestone and momentum point attainment. *CCRC Research Tools.* Issue No. 2.

Levens, M. 2010. *Marketing: Defined, Explained, Applied.* Upper Saddle River, NJ: Pearson Education, Inc.

Lincoln, C. 2009. Courageous conversations: Achieving the dream and the importance of student success. *Change.* January/February: 24–41. Available at: <www.changemag.org/Archives/Back Issues/January-February 2009/full-achieving-dream.html>.

Marklein, M.B. 2009. College recruiters are Twittering, too. *USA Today.* April 29, News/Education section. Available at: <www.usatoday.com/news/education/2009-04-29-admissions-twitter_N.htm>.

Martin, D. 2009. Update: return of the Twitter quitters. *Nielsen Wire.* April 30, Online And Mobile section. Available at: <http://blog.nielsen.com/nielsenwire/online_mobile/update-return-of-the-twitter-quitters/>.

McClenney, K.M. 2004. *Keeping America's Promise: Challenges for Community Colleges* (leadership abstracts). Phoenix, AZ: League for Innovation.

McGiboney, M. 2009. Twitter's tweet smell of success. *Nielsen Wire.* March 18, Online and Mobile section. Available at: <http://blog.nielsen.com/nielsenwire/online_mobile/twitters-tweet-smell-of-success/>.

Miller, J.R. 2009. "Twitterjacking"—Identity theft in 140 characters or less. Fox News. April 30, Scitech section. Available at: <www.foxnews.com/story/0,2933,518480,00.html>.

Mitchell, G.N., and C.L. Grafton. 1985. Comparative study of reverse transfer, lateral transfer, and first-time community college students. *Community/Junior College Quarterly.* 9: 273–280.

Nah, F.H., and S. Delgado. 2006. Critical success factors for enterprise resource planning implementation and upgrade. *The Journal of Computer Information Systems.* 46(5): 99–113.

National Coalition for Homeless Veterans. *Effective Community Collaboration.* Washington, DC: National Coalition for Homeless Veterans. Retrieved July 23, 2009 from: <www.nchv.org/docs/Collaboration%20 6.28c.pdf>. [C5]

National Governors Association and the National Association of State Budget Officers. 2006. *The Fiscal Survey of States, December 2006.* Washington, DC: National Association of State Budget Officers.

Noel Levitz. 2009. *Retooling the Enrollment Funnel: Strategies and Metrics for a New Era* (white paper). Available at: <www.noellevitz.com/NR/rdonlyres/B0D6DFDA-5D2A-41D9-AB9C-DCEF22989F5A/0/Re toolingTheEnrollmentFunnel0109.pdf>.

Nora Ganim Barnes, P. 2007. *Reaching the Wired Gengeration: How Social Media is Changing College Admission* (2007 NACAC discussion paper). Arlington, VA: National Association for College Admission Counseling.

Northouse, P.G. 2001. *Leadership: Theory and Practice.* Thousand Oaks, CA: Sage Publications, Inc.

O'Donoghue, T., and K. Punch. 2003. *Qualitative Educational Research in Action: Doing and Reflecting.* London: Routledge.

Ostrow, A. 2009. Social networking more popular than email. *Mashable.* March 9. Available at: <http://mashable.com/2009/03/09/social-networking-more-popular-than-email/>.

Palmer, J.C., M. Ludwig, and L. Stapleton. 1994. *At What Point do Community College Students Transfer to Baccalaureate-Granting Institutions? Evidence from a 13-State Study*. Washington, DC: American Council on Education. Available at: <www.eric.ed.gov/ERICWebPortal/contentdelivery/servlet/ERICServlet?accno=ED373844 >.

Papa, J. 2002. *College Admissions: Operations and Management* (workshop). AACRAO Annual Meeting Minneapolis. April 14.

Pascarella, E.T., and P.T. Terenzini. 1991. *How College Affects Students: Findings and Insights from Twenty Years of Research*. San Francisco: Jossey-Bass.

Peter, K., and C.D. Carroll. 2005. *The Road Less Traveled? Students Who Enroll in Multiple Institutions*. NCES Publication No. 2005157. Washington, DC: National Center for Education Statistics. Available at: <http://nces.ed.gov/pubs2005/2005157.pdf>.

Piland, W.E. 1995. Community college transfer students who earn bachelor's degrees. *Community College Review*. 23(3): 35–44.

Popkin, H. 2009. *Twitter gets you fired in 140 characters or less*. *MSNBC*. March 23, Technotica section. Available at: <www.msnbc.msn.com/id/29796962/>.

Porter, J., M. Hogan, and M. Gebel. 2000. *The Non-Linear Transfer Student: The Case of Transfer, Returning Transfer, Re-Transfer, and Co-Enrollment*. Paper presented at the Annual Forum of the Association for Institutional Research, Cincinnati, OH.

Provasnik, S., and M. Planty. 2008. *Community Colleges: Special Supplement to The 2008 Condition of Education*. (NCES Publication No. 2008–033). Washington, DC: National Center for Education Statistics. Available at: <http://nces.ed.gov/pubs2008/2008033.pdf >.

Quanty, M.B., R.W. Dixon, and D.R. Ridley. 1996. *The Course-Based Model of Transfer Success: An Action-Oriented Research Paradigm*. Paper presented at the Annual Conference of the Southeastern Association for Community College Research, Panama City, FL.

Rawlinson, J. How to use Twitter for customer service. *Return Customer* (blog). January 14, 2009. Retrieved May 7, 2009 from: <www.returncustomer.com/2009/01/14/how-to-use-twitter-for-customer-service/>.

Ryan, J.F. 2007. The other leaky pipeline: repairing our research infrastructure to enhance post secondary student success. *Enrollment Management Journal*. 1(1): 10–22.

Sanchez, J.R., and F.S. Laanan. 1997. *What is it Worth? The Economic Value of Obtaining a Certificate or Associate Degree from California Community Colleges*. Paper presented at the Annual Conference of the California Association for Institutional Research, San Francisco, CA.

Serban, A. 2008. *A Qualitative Study of Two-to-Four Year Transfer Practices in California Community Colleges*. Berkeley, CA: Research and Planning Group for California Community Colleges. Available at: <http://rpgroup.org/documents/TLC_Cross_Case_Analysis.pdf>.

Sevier, Robert A. 2003. *An Integrated Marketing Workbook for College and Universities*. Hiawatha, IA: Strategy Publishing.

Sharp, K.H. 2007. *A Study of Community College Cost Structures*. Ph.D. dissertation, The University of Arizona.

Smith, C. 2008. *Finding the academic context: The SEM role for faculty*. Washington, DC: AACRAO Consulting Services.

Snyder, T.D. 2009. *Mini-Digest of Education Statistics, 2008* (NCES Publication No. 2009021). Washington, DC: National Center for Education Statistics. Available at: <http://nces.ed.gov/pubs2009/2009021.pdf>.

Society for College and University Planning. 2009. Academic planning. In *Pathways to Planning* (online guide). Available at: <www1.scup.org/resources/pathways/pathways.php?id=plan-academic>.

Swail, W.S., R. Mullen, H. Gardner, and J. Reed. 2008. *Engaging Faculty and Staff: An Imperative for Fostering Retention, Advising, and Smart Borrowing*. Round Rock, TX: Educational Policy Institute.

UCLA Online Institute for Cyberspace Law and Policy. 2001. *The Digital Millennium Copyright Act—Overview*. Retrieved May 13, 2009 from: <www.gseis.ucla.edu/iclp/dmca1.htm>.

Vaughan, G. 2005. (Over)selling the community college: What price access? *Chronicle of Higher Education*. 52(10): B12.

Ward, J. 2005. Enrollment management: Key elements for building and implementing an enrollment plan. *College and University.* 80(4): 7–12.

Whiteside, R. 1998. *Maximizing Enrollment Health: The SEM Rx.* PowerPoint presentation SEM VIII Conference. Aspen, CO.

Wikipedia. 2009. *Partnership.* Retrieved April 11, from: <http://en.wikipedia.org/wiki/Partnership>.

Wilkens, J. 2009. UCSD makes admissions error—again. *The San Diego Union-Tribune.* May 6. Available at: <www3.signonsandiego.com/stories/2009/may/06/1n6ucsd002342-ucsd-makes-admissions-error-8211-aga/>.

Wirt, J., S. Choy, P. Rooney, S. Provasnik, A. Sen, and R. Tobin. 2004. *The Condition of Education 2004* (NCES Publication No. 2004077). Washington, DC: National Center for Education Statistics. Available at: <http://nces.ed.gov/pubs2004/2004077.pdf>.

Worona, S.L. 2009. Director of Policy and Networking Programs EDUCAUSE. (W. Kilgore, Interviewer). May 13.

Zeiss, C.D. 2001. *True Partnership: Revolutionary Thinking About Relating to Others.* San Francisco: Berrett-Koehler Publishing, Inc.